I0754918

Healing the Success Wound

Healing the Success Wound

ALIGN YOUR AMBITION,
FIND LASTING CAREER FULFILLMENT,
AND END THE CYCLE OF NEVER-ENOUGH

BROOKE TAYLOR

New York Boston

This book is not intended as a substitute for medical advice of physicians. The reader should regularly consult a physician in all matters relating to his or her health, and particularly in respect of any symptoms that may require diagnosis or medical attention.

Balance
Hachette Book Group
1290 Avenue of the Americas
New York, NY 10104
GCP-Balance.com
@GCPBalance

First Edition: May 2026

Balance is an imprint of Grand Central Publishing. The Balance name and logo are registered trademarks of Hachette Book Group, Inc.

Print book interior design by Bart Dawson.

Library of Congress Control Number: 2026931250

ISBNs: 9780306836107 (hardcover); 9780306836121 (ebook)

Printed in the United States of America

LSC-C

Printing 1, 2026

Dedicated to James, who, from the moment we met, reminded me I am enough.

And to Crosby, just for being you.

There is a vitality, a life force, an energy, a quickening that is translated through you into action, and because there is only one of you in all time, this expression is unique. And if you block it, it will never exist through any other medium and it will be lost. The world will not have it. It is not your business to determine how good it is nor how valuable nor how it compares with other expressions. It is your business to keep it yours clearly and directly to keep the channel open. You do not even have to believe in yourself or your work. You have to keep yourself open and aware to the urges that motivate you.

Keep the channel open.

No artist is pleased. No satisfaction whatever at any time. There is only a queer, divine dissatisfaction, a blessed unrest that keeps us marching and makes us more alive than the others.

—Martha Graham

CONTENTS

Healing the Success Wound

AUTHOR'S NOTE

The client stories shared in these pages are fictional and do not depict any specific person or situation. Rather, they are composites drawn from themes and experiences I've encountered in sessions with hundreds of women over the last eight years. While the details have been changed, the emotions, thought patterns, and dilemmas reflect the real inner lives of many working women. The client session is a sacred space, and I will never relay its exact contents.

Additionally, some of the exercises and topics in this book may evoke painful feelings or past experiences. I encourage you to address this with a trained therapist. The practices and recommendations in this book are not a substitute for psychotherapy. I don't present myself as a therapist or clinician. Instead, I draw on the insights of trusted experts in those fields and refer to their work throughout, while sharing what I've learned through coaching and lived experience.

INTRODUCTION

The Empty Cup Within

On an autumn afternoon in New York City's Financial District, I sat across from Sutton, a vice president at a major bank next door. This was our first coaching session. She'd requested to meet during her lunch break, the only hour in the long day where she could take a few minutes for herself.

Sutton took a final sip of her second coffee and held the empty paper cup. "It's like I have this empty cup inside of me," she started, shaking it for effect. Imagine a cup containing all of one's career accomplishments, big and small—well-deserved promotions, positive feedback from a manager, the satisfaction of finally cracking a tough model. Sutton's cup should have been overflowing, but it has a leak in the bottom. "It's never full," she said. "I am never full."

Despite being consistently ranked in the top 15 percent of employees at her company, Sutton always felt behind and "racing to catch up." To what or whom, she didn't know. "The empty-cup feeling is awful, but it motivates me," she explained. After all, she wouldn't want to lose her drive. But why was she feeling so inadequate?

She adjusted her glasses. Her voice wavering, she continued, "Well, I can't hold on to the pride of these accomplishments, because the cup instantly drains and demands to be filled again."

No matter how much she accomplished, no matter what level she achieved, it never felt like enough. *She* never felt like enough.

Sutton's metaphor wasn't unique. As a career coach to highly ambitious women, I've heard some version of the empty-cup feeling thousands of times—in my group coaching programs at companies like Google and McKinsey, in client sessions in my private practice, and in workshops for women leaders around the globe. I have worked with over six thousand of these "Unfulfilled Achievers." An Unfulfilled Achiever is someone who has been going above and beyond her whole life yet doubts she'll ever reach the heights of success she craves. Nor do her achievements bring her any sense of peace. To the contrary, anxiety is ever present. She cannot separate her identity from work and relies upon approval for motivation. Highly competent, she's always declaring, "I'll figure it out." Her brilliant mind can solve most problems in her life, except this one: how to feel fulfilled in her career and believe that she is enough.

If that's you too, hi. This book is for you. You're part of a generation of women more ambitious than ever and yet more unsatisfied than ever.

According to McKinsey's 2023 *Women in the Workplace* study, 80 percent of women want to be promoted, rising to 88 percent for women of color. Three in four women under thirty years old aspire to reach senior leadership.[1] But the journey to the top often comes with a price: Women in positions of power in the workplace experience higher rates of burnout, anxiety, and depression than both their male counterparts and women with less authority.[2] Structural inequalities like the gender pay gap and unconscious bias are significant drivers of this dissatisfaction for women at work.

Yet after thousands of coaching sessions, I noticed something deeper. My clients described an insatiable need to achieve and to prove their worth not just as an employee but as a person. Their mood, identity, and sense of self all would rise and fall with their career wins and losses.

Determined to bring words and data to this phenomenon, I went through hundreds of pages of client notes, spanning more than 280 individuals, to look for trends. These women worked in corporate, nonprofit, and public sector roles in countries such as the United States, Australia, the United Kingdom, Singapore, Saudi Arabia, Nigeria, and France. Some consistent themes emerged: In childhood, they learned that achievement brought attention, praise, and love. In their perpetual attempt to live up to a specific standard of goodness set by their parents and cultural upbringing, they internalized the belief that *their* goodness was earned.

This created a wound on their psyche, an underlying pain derived from not feeling worthy exactly as they are. Now as adults with impressive careers, they do not feel safe or in control unless they are constantly producing and winning approval.

This core wound is what I call the *success wound*: the false belief that your worthiness of love and belonging is contingent upon what you produce, achieve, or do rather than the inherent goodness of who you are. Ultimately, it is a feeling of inadequacy that influences how we react to ourselves, to our work, and the world around us. The empty-cup feeling—that haunting feeling of never being enough, never measuring up, never getting it just right—that's your success wound.

In the workplace, women develop coping mechanisms to defend against this gnawing inadequacy. In my research, I've found that there are five primary ways Unfulfilled Achievers attempt to cover up the hurt of their success wound and live up to incredibly high, often unrealistic, standards. I've given names to these archetypes:

- The Grinder: She overworks to prove her value through constant doing.
- The Pleaser: She's the team player who is always doing for others to maintain harmony and her reputation as agreeable.
- The Hider: She avoids risk by staying within her comfort zone.
- The Seeker: She searches endlessly for the next job, the next promotion, or external validation.
- The Work Hard, Play Hard: She pushes to perform and numbs unwanted emotions in unhealthy ways, calling it "balance."

The very strategies that feel like success (overworking, pleasing, proving) are actually fueling burnout, anxiety, depression, workaholism, and total disengagement from work. According to market sizing done by the Training Industry in 2024, companies spent over $397 billion a year globally on leadership development to fix these exact issues ($184.9 billion of that spend is in the United States).[3] Yet these programs often fail to move the needle. Why? Because they fail to address the emotional root causes of poor leadership: low self-efficacy, a lack of self-awareness, and emotional dysregulation—all of which comes from their employees' success wounds.

In addition, more and more employees are questioning the role of work and traditional markers of achievement. According to a 2024 study conducted by PwC, after a fair paycheck, today's workforce values fulfillment and purpose at work. Yet neither employee nor employer can provide that sense of purpose.[4] This book will provide both an explanation to the question of why you're feeling so unsatisfied at work and a plan for what to do about it.

MY UNFULFILLED ACHIEVER STORY

I know the success wound so intimately because it nearly ruined my promising career at Google and stole both my fulfillment and my sense of self.

As a teenager growing up in Silicon Valley, I had many benefits of privilege, and with them came a tremendous amount of pressure. I quickly got the message that I had to be not just above average, but extraordinary and accomplished. I noticed that the better my grades were, the more praise I received from teachers, my parents, and even my friends. The opposite was also true; a B– was met with a question ("Well, did you try your best?") and the quiet suggestion that I wasn't "living up to my potential." Working harder was the only answer. I came by my success wound honestly.

Achievement pressure is not unique to students in Silicon Valley—it's everywhere. Regardless of the childhood circumstances, nearly all my clients speak of the weight of this pressure. In her book *Never Enough: When Achievement Culture Becomes Toxic—and What We Can Do About It*, author and journalist Jennifer Breheny Wallace reported on a national parenting survey she conducted with the Harvard Graduate School of Education. She interviewed parents coast to coast, studying the impact of achievement culture on children, asking them to what extent they agreed with statements like "Parents in my community generally agree that getting into a selective college is one of the most important ingredients to later-life happiness" (73 percent agreed) and "I wish today's childhood was less stressful for my kids" (87 percent agreed).[5] These parenting philosophies reflect a cultural value of achievement and the pressure to meet an ever-rising standard of productivity and excellence, to which none of us is immune.

As the daughter of parents of the second-wave feminist movement, which expanded opportunities for women in the workplace, I was raised on the encouraging idea that I could do anything I set my mind to. However, in practice, "anything" I *could* be was a very narrow expectation of what I *should* be: high-achieving. If the sky was the limit, then we were expected to climb into positions of power traditionally occupied by men: CEO, president, entrepreneur. The expectation was *Sure, be whatever you want, just as long as you are the best in a respected field.*

I spent the next thirteen years attempting to be "the best" in the eyes of anyone who perceived me. By age twenty-four, I worked at Google and managed a portfolio of clients that spent over $80 million in advertising. At parties or on dates, I couldn't wait for people to ask what I did for work to make their eyes widen with surprise at my answer. "I work for Google." I hoped this brand-name, buzz-worthy employer would protect me from being seen as completely ordinary (read: average, unremarkable, not enough). I imagined people—no one in particular, just people in general—responding with a blend of envy and admiration: *Wow, she really has it all.* In my vocabulary, *envy* and *admiration* were synonyms for connection and love, and there was no limit to the amount of both required to fill that empty cup within.

I developed a mask for my business self: a Work Hard, Play Hard persona, which is one of the five types of Unfulfilled Achievers we will discuss throughout this book. I aspired to be the hard-charging professional who was both the life of the office and the party, effortlessly competent, agreeable, and admired. In our corporate culture, happy hours were an unspoken requirement for advancement, a way to curry favor in a system where management clearly played favorites. I wanted to belong to this team of high achievers more than to myself, and working hard and playing hard was my way to fit in.

These very strategies that I thought would make me successful started to make me sick. My week went something like this: Monday through Thursday, I poured myself into work where every client presentation, every email response, every answer I gave to every question felt like a referendum on my competence and my value. By Friday, I was so depleted that I would drink to numb the emptiness, only to wake up on Sunday feeling exhausted, demoralized, anxious, and lost. As the Monday morning sun rose, bringing with it a familiar mix of adrenaline and dread, I'd peel myself out of bed, hoping this week would be different.

A car can only go full throttle for so long before it runs out of gas. I wanted to scream all the time, hoping someone would notice and rip my foot off the accelerator. A part of me wanted to keep pushing, while another was praying for absolution from this ride that never ended.

Then, suddenly, this cycle came to a screeching halt. I found myself in a situation I never expected: I experienced sexual harassment by my direct manager. The next day, I walked through the Google New York office doors as I had thousands of times and shakily put my laptop down on my desk. The shame and nausea turned my stomach and crawled up my throat, gripping it tightly. Instead of seeing this event as the abuse of power that it was, I blamed myself. *How could I be so stupid? I can never report this, ever.* Reporting the harassment, I believed then, might threaten my status at a company whose brand equity I borrowed as my own. Without Google, who was I? And without my bosses' approval, what chance did I have at rising in the ranks or feeling good about myself? I was up for promotion and did not want to anger or embarrass the very people who could grant me the approval and prestige I needed.

And so I decided not to report the harassment. I chose to protect my manager and the culture he represented instead of protecting myself. My silence was deafening and demoralizing. In retrospect, I acknowledge that other imbalances of power were at play. However, this event also highlighted a dependence that I could no longer ignore.

It was the first moment where I could see myself, my choices, and this toxic cycle clearly. I realized I needed an entirely new relationship with my job, and a new way of seeing my value. At the time, I didn't know anyone else struggling with the same issues. Years later, I learned I was surrounded by other corporate women wrestling with their relationship to their careers and workplace culture. I couldn't find a solution or resource that combined inner healing with practical actions for working sustainably and effectively within a corporation.

So I created my own.

I researched and experimented with new working methods that brought confidence and power instead of fear. I started to heal the hurt parts of me from childhood that believed she wasn't enough unless she was constantly achieving. I discovered an inner resource, what I like to call the True Self, that was innately confident. This part of me already knew who she was, what she wanted, and how to work sustainably; I just had to ask her for advice. From this place, I adopted a new mindset of finding my value in my presence, not my productivity. Instead of trying to do the most at work, I pursued only my most essential priorities (which you will also do in Chapter 7).

This is aligned ambition, the state of fulfillment, satisfaction, and power that comes from following the direction of your True Self over the directions of your success wound. Surprisingly, I didn't have to leave Google to make a change. Instead, I landed a new job on an exciting new team at Google, received my highest performance rating, and was promoted within eighteen months without burning out. Work set me into a state of flow and fulfillment. People began to notice my newfound confidence and career trajectory. Two years later, during the #MeToo movement, I had the courage to do what I couldn't before: I reported the harassment and took a stand for my younger self. Instead of being a hamster wheel, work became an arena for my growth. I was finally working in the sustainable, values-aligned way I'd always dreamed of.

One day in August 2018, about two and a half years into my aligned ambition experiment, I was on a career panel in collaboration between Google, Kate Spade, and Girls Who Code. I went off script and talked about my methods for finding career satisfaction. It struck a chord. Afterward, a woman nodding and beaming from the audience asked if I offered coaching. She became my first client, and my coaching business was born. The pillars of aligned ambition—a new way of feeling, a new way of thinking, and a new way of working—could generate replicable results for others. My clients went back into their workplaces as changed, happier people. Their friends and colleagues saw the transformation and said to them, "I want whatever you have," and my practice grew. After years of research, experimentation, and scaling these methods in my group coaching program called Healing the Success Wound, I'm happy to report that aligned ambition is teachable and learnable.

ALIGNED AMBITION IS A NEW WAY OF WORKING THAT WORKS

Today, I have guided over six thousand women to a new way of working that works. Dozens of companies (like Google and Uber) and women's organizations have hired me to talk to their employees about how to find career fulfillment from the inside out. These aren't radical ideas anymore; there is an understanding among many corporate leaders that better business outcomes arise from employee engagement and motivation. For companies, my workshops and talks have resulted in a 150 percent increase in retention (saving thousands of dollars in recruiting and onboarding costs) and a 400 percent increase in critical leadership skills, as measured in pre- and post-program surveys.

Practicing aligned ambition doesn't mean putting your career aspirations aside. Rather, it leads to faster and more sustainable goal attainment. My clients have doubled their salaries, started businesses, and secured funding; they have published their memoirs, landed their dream jobs, and pivoted their careers entirely at age forty-five. They got these results not because they were lucky but because they bravely challenged outdated notions of success that were no longer serving them, followed the steps in this book, and started listening to their True Selves.

OUR JOURNEY AHEAD

This book explores the roots—and the reach—of the success wound in professional women and offers a path to heal it fully and forever. Together, we will explore how fulfillment in both career and life is only possible through adopting a new work paradigm outside the prevailing culture.

We won't sugarcoat the truth. We'll name the systems (capitalism, patriarchy, achievement culture) that keep so many women disconnected from their power.

You will also hear stories from other professional women about how they found their aligned ambition through the steps in this book. From investment bankers in Boston to software engineers in San Francisco to business owners in rural Texas. Daughters of determined immigrants and daughters of small-business owners, working mothers, single mothers, and women without children.

Though the details of their lives may look different, their internal landscapes feel the same. They all grappled with their relationship to work and their relationship to themselves. Whether it's grinding to escape the financial insecurity of their childhood or feeling lost and wondering if they'll ever find the thing that makes their heart sing, they all strive for the same goals: fulfillment, meaningful work, and authentic belonging. The practices in these pages offer you a path there.

WHAT YOU'LL FIND IN THIS BOOK

This book is divided into three parts. First, you'll uncover the psychological and cultural roots of your success wound and identify your Unfulfilled Achiever type. Then you'll learn how to reconnect with your True Self and shift how you feel, think, and work. Finally, you'll step into aligned ambition, a more powerful and sustainable way of being at work and in your life.

I hope that this book can be a career guide that you return to in small moments when your confidence is waning, or in larger, pivotal times like after maternity leave or a promotion when you need to be reminded how to navigate your career from the inside out. For example, if you're falling into people-pleasing tendencies because you just started a new job, you can revisit the Pleaser archetype and find ways to realign with your inner confidence. If your success wound flares up and you return to comparing yourself with others, you can turn to the "new way of feeling" in Chapter 5 and be guided through witnessing and releasing these old feelings and returning to a state of clarity. These tools are exactly that—tools that are timeless and cannot be taken from you.

Together, we will hold your ambition in one hand and your self-worth in another, and you will believe wholeheartedly that you are ambitious and whole and worthy. Full stop. You are worthy of achieving your big dreams, and you deserve the satisfaction of your accomplishments. You may choose to build an empire, or you may choose to eat bonbons on the couch all day. The choice is yours. Because you are still worthy of love and belonging. You are, and have always been, whole. You are enough, right now and forever.

By the end, I hope you have a new way of working and being in the world that unlocks your greatest power. This way, you can create and achieve anything *you* truly want while also feeling free, fulfilled, and enough.

Aligned ambition matters. This isn't just about more women in leadership. It's about more women in leadership who are fully themselves—tuned in, turned on, and leading from truth. That can't happen if we're still trying to win at a game that was never built for us. Healing the success wound is a radical act of self-care and world care. We need your aligned ambition, and we need you.

To innovate is to produce something new by applying a different method. My guess is that you've been using your head to approach your career—endlessly analyzing the options, consulting expert opinions—and still coming up short. We are going to innovate the space of professional development and career satisfaction by starting at the heart. We'll look within to the part of us that has wisdom and guidance beyond career "best practices." If you're willing to have an open mind and an open heart, then you're ready to get started.

This book is the one I needed most when I was burned out, unsure of my worth, and wondering if there was any alternative. I didn't just want to survive my career. I wanted to feel like I was thriving in it. That's what I hope this book helps you find, too.

PART 1

THE UNFULFILLED ACHIEVER

CHAPTER 1

NEVER ENOUGH

The Origins of Your Success Wound

"So sorry for being late." It was 2:02 p.m., yet Talia, dashing through the doorway for her coaching session, was already feeling behind. She was a rising star at a fast-growing media company, recently promoted into the director of advertising role.

"We talked about this," I said gently. "It's okay to give yourself a moment between meetings." Talia took a deep breath—her first of the day—and placed her Diet Coke on the desk—her second of the day.

"I'm just not cutting it, and everyone knows it," she lamented.

When I asked how she came to that conclusion, she replied, "Last week, I presented our annual plan, and there were so many questions and so much doubt in the room. That shouldn't happen to someone with 'director' in their title." She sighed. "A real leader should command respect. Have a vision that everyone can rally behind."

Anytime I hear the word *should* I listen for the invisible standards my clients hold themselves to. We all have a mental image of a successful professional woman that we constantly strive for and compare ourselves to. Our very own collage of *shoulds* pasted together, forming an alluring promise of happiness. This mirage is ever-shifting and always out of reach. No matter how hard we try to live up to it, we come up empty-handed, hustling to prove our value. In the gap between this vision and reality lies a perception of inadequacy.

I asked Talia how her own mental image of a successful director affected her daily working life. She took a sip of her Diet Coke and thought for a moment. "I'm always wondering if I am living up to the image of a 'good' executive, especially as a Black woman. I would hate to be seen as difficult, but equally I don't want to be a doormat, or—worst of all—disappointing. I'm always stepping in to help people, even if it's not in my job scope. My schedule's chaotic. I'm racing from meeting to meeting. But what I'm racing to catch up to, I don't know."

I echoed back to her, "Always behind. Never enough."

"Exactly," she said, nodding.

These thoughts reverberate throughout the minds of millions of working women. A 2023 study from the Conference Board on job satisfaction in the United States found that women, from entry level to executive, reported significantly lower career satisfaction than their male peers.[1] When considering this fog of discontent—this problem with no name—that plagues my clients, I was reminded of Betty Friedan's seminal book *The Feminine*

Mystique. In 1963, Friedan observed a rising dissatisfaction among white American housewives. Many women were not content living in service of their children and husbands, forced to give up other educational and professional aspirations. They packed lunches and drove car pool, secretly wondering, *Is this all life has to offer?*

Today, despite the incredible leaps in opportunities for women in political, social, and professional rights, women are still asking themselves the same question: *Is this really it?* This dissatisfaction has taken a new shape. Women still contend with a cultural ideal of success rather than their own. But now, instead of buying the image of the happy housewife, they are sold the image of the professional woman who can easily do it all. The having-it-all portrait might look slightly different from person to person depending upon one's background, upbringing, and preferences. Some want to be the prestigious achiever who is envied for working at the hottest "it" company. Others seek the perfect balance between family, work, and well-being, never missing a beat. Some idolize the "Partner" title so they can finally be considered a leader, while others fantasize about being the effortless entrepreneur who enjoys both their flexible schedule and consistent revenue growth.

While there are as many different ideals as there are people, the habit is the same: attempting to emulate the successful working woman we think we *should* be instead of who we actually want to be. And when we fail to emulate her, we question our worth, value, and competence, instead of questioning the culture that sold us this impossible standard in the first place.

The inadequacy stems from the same place: the success wound. The *success wound* is the term I've coined for the invisible pain that comes from mistaking one's career for self-worth. It's an unconscious habit of tying your worthiness of love and sense of belonging to what you produce, achieve, and do, rather than who you are. Sure, you logically know that *you* aren't your job. You know that real happiness isn't found in a title or a salary. But there's still a belief, deep down, that says you do need to prove your value.

Here are the kinds of sentiments I typically hear in sessions with my clients:

- "I'm only as good as my last piece of feedback."
- "I could always be doing more."
- "I feel lost and constantly question if I'm on the right career path."
- "The wrong look from my boss can send me reeling for days."
- "I have this constant inner voice that says, *If you relax, you'll lose your edge.*"
- "I have big dreams but fear of failure stops me before I even start."
- "I've reached the pinnacle of my career. It's what I wanted, I should be happy, so why do I feel empty?"
- "I constantly feel unsafe, as if my money or job could be taken from me at any moment."
- "I'm always onto the next thing, so I never fully enjoy what I've just accomplished."

I shared this list with Talia, who nodded. "Yep, that's me. I've had all those thoughts." I explained that her success wound was to blame. "Not my perfectionism? Or imposter syndrome?" she questioned. The success wound often gets misdiagnosed as both. They are related but distinct concepts. While imposter syndrome makes you question your competence, and perfectionism is the tendency to demand an impossibly ideal standard, the success wound is the underlying belief that you are only worthy when you're succeeding. It's the hidden engine driving those other struggles, and healing it requires a different approach.

In the last six years, I have collected over two thousand responses to an intake form completed by professional women seeking coaching. In it, I ask what three primary factors are preventing their career satisfaction. Because respondents typically selected three options, the percentages here reflect how frequently each issue was chosen rather than totaling to 100 percent. Sixty percent blamed their perfectionism, 40 percent pointed to their imposter syndrome, 25 percent said it's their procrastination, 55 percent reported lack of boundaries, and 65 percent blamed being in the wrong job. But these are not the real cause. Rather, they are symptoms of an unconscious habit of tying your identity to your professional outcomes. In Talia's case, her self-esteem was pinned to how the other members of her leadership team perceived her. No wonder her natural impulse was to make things perfect, go back on her boundaries, and procrastinate the tasks she lacked expertise in.

WHERE DOES THE SUCCESS WOUND COME FROM?

Here's the thing: You weren't born with your success wound. Rather it slowly developed over time. It may have begun early, socialized within you by your cultural upbringing—the specific values that govern your society, community, and family. While having a success wound is not our fault, healing it is our responsibility. The first step in healing is to understand the diagnosis, to examine the origins of our discontent.

The Early Years

The success wound can form from early experiences that link achievement with self-worth. When children receive love and approval mainly for their accomplishments and desirable outcomes, they begin to equate achievement with being valuable. The wound is reinforced by early experiences—a teacher's criticism ("You can do better than that"), a parent's comparison ("Your sister did it, why can't you?"), or the quiet drip of disapproval ("Did you *really* try your best?"). Children also pick up on what is unsaid, such as the example their parents set, how they talk about their own work, and the subtleties of how parents react with a forced smile or genuine pride.

Physician Gabor Maté suggests that children have two primary needs: authenticity and attachment. Authenticity is the need to be who we are, our True Self, while attachment is the need to feel connected and loved by caregivers. When attachment is threatened or withdrawn, even in small ways, children often blame themselves, thinking, *There's something wrong with me*. Their self-worth and innate belief that they are lovable is diminished. Research shows that children who feel less loved and connected grow into adults with low self-worth.[2]

Children look to adults and the world around them to understand goodness: what's optimal, socially acceptable, and appropriate behavior. "Success" is not only an ability to achieve a goal; it is our determination of this goodness and our ability to live up to it. I remember walking through the hallways of my school in sixth grade seeing the banners of elite colleges hung prominently: Yale, Princeton, Cal Berkeley, Stanford. In my eleven-year-old brain, the message was clear: This is what success looks like after graduating from high school, and everything you do from now until then is for the purpose of being admitted to an elite college.

When we observe how success is defined, we start to measure our worth by that definition. Not just our behaviors or talents, but us as human beings. In an article titled "Students in High-Achieving Schools Are Now Named an 'At-Risk' Group, Study Says," author Jennifer Breheny Wallace explains: "When a child's sense of self-worth is dependent on what they achieve, it can lead to anxiety and depression."[3] From age twelve, I struggled with anxiety that came with the intense pressure I felt to keep up in an academically rigorous environment. I also had bouts of depression that arose from a perpetual sense that I wasn't smart enough to belong to one of the universities on those banners.

Years later, my clients shared their own stories of other kinds of pressure they experienced to live up to the cultural ideals of success held for them by their parents and communities. When we explored the origins of her success wound in childhood, Talia shared, "I was in classes from 7 a.m. until 3 p.m., then chess club or basketball practice, and back home to make dinner for my siblings while my dad worked late. I felt like I had to perform well in every area of my life in order to one day get a scholarship and to make things easier at home." This habit of responding to what a parent or person in power wants us to be is carried throughout our working lives.

Consequently, as adults, our psyches may shield our success wound in the form of compensating behaviors and personality traits to keep us accepted, approved of, and seen as competent and in control. These are the parts of us that come to the rescue when we are stressed, out of our comfort zone, and feeling threatened or afraid. These behaviors—and their related archetypes—include:

- Working relentlessly, using productivity as a defense against feelings of inadequacy, striving to prove their worth through constant achievement. (The Grinder)
- Avoiding visibility or not taking on high-profile projects to protect against the potential failure, rejection, and the ensuing shame. (The Hider)
- Continually searching for new achievements—the next job, the next promotion, the next big client—hoping that the next one will finally bring validation and acceptance. (The Seeker)
- Sacrificing personal needs to meet others' expectations; putting the needs of a boss, colleague, client, or direct report ahead of your own in order to gain acceptance. (The Pleaser)
- Working intensely and "balancing" it with unhealthy escapism as a temporary relief from the pressure to achieve. (The Work Hard, Play Hard)

Over time, the more we rely on these behaviors, the more we confuse them for who we are ("I'm a hustle and make-it-happen person"; "I'm such a people pleaser"). This further separates you from your authenticity.

The Psychology of the Success Wound

Your inner Unfulfilled Achiever is just one part of you, not your whole story. Within each of us lies a True Self, a part that inherently knows who she is, what she wants, where she's going, and why. Though I refer to the True Self as an intuitive guide, and a counterpart to the inner Unfulfilled Achiever, I didn't invent its concept. Multiple psychological frameworks describe this concept of *True Self*, or simply *Self*, as part of the psyche. In Internal Family Systems (IFS) therapy, developed by therapist Richard Schwartz, the Self is characterized by qualities including the 8 C's: compassion, curiosity, clarity, creativity, calm, confidence, courage, and connectedness; and the 4 P's: presence, playfulness, perseverance, and perspective.[4] This part of you is innate. She doesn't need to be built; she is already within you offering wisdom beyond your logical mind.

Just as an acorn carries the blueprint for an oak tree, your True Self holds the path to your fullest expression in life and work. She knows how to guide your career and inform your workday with clarity, confidence, and fulfillment. And the best part? She can never be broken. Even when hidden behind your success wound's negative chatter, she's still there, during stressful weeks, hunkered down at your desk or racing between meetings. She might be quiet, but she's indeed waiting behind the scenes, ready to help you work from your innate confidence and strong presence. That's the purpose of this book: to help you return to her.

Lasting fulfillment is only possible when working from the True Self. In my coaching programs and workshops, I see yearning in the eyes of participants when I introduce the concept of the True Self and the possibility of working *from* her. One woman, Suzanne, shared, "I know there's a True Self within me, but it's been years since I've accessed her." Suzanne said that she appears fleetingly but feels impossible to grasp, let alone harness, "especially in my busy schedule and corporate environment." Many women nod in agreement, noting they experience their intuition during meditation, playing with their kids, or in nature, but rarely at work.

A CULTURE OF "NOT ENOUGH"

Any conversation about our dissatisfaction as working women would be incomplete without examining the broader norms and expectations that contribute to it. As a cisgender white woman, I acknowledge that my perspectives and experiences within capitalism and patriarchy are privileged. I acknowledge that there are many entrenched systems of oppression facing women and underrepresented persons globally. Here, I am talking about a few examples at the intersection of patriarchy and capitalism that diminish women's perceived value of themselves and feed the success wound.

The Morality of Hard Work

There were days I felt guilty for leaving the office, even though it was after 5 p.m. Sometimes I would finish my work faster than my colleagues. I questioned my character. Was I lazy? Would my colleagues think I wasn't a dedicated teammate if I didn't stay late? Sometimes I stayed at my desk longer just to show that I was diligent, even though I wasn't producing better work. There were other times when I received more praise for a project that came more effortlessly than work that I agonized over. I brushed off the accolades, figuring I didn't really deserve them if the work hadn't been challenging.

My instincts were correct: People *do* associate positive character traits with those who work harder. Social psychologist Azim Shariff conducted a study in which participants were presented with two hypothetical individuals, Justin and Mark. Both work in a factory making widgets at the same rate: six widgets per hour. Justin finds the work easy and requires minimal effort, while Mark finds the work difficult and effortful. When asked to evaluate these individuals, participants rated Justin as more competent due to his ease of work. However, notably, they perceived Mark, who put in more effort, as a more moral person, assigning him character traits like "responsible," "principled," and "trustworthy." This phenomenon is called effort moralization: in which people tend to attribute higher moral value to putting in effort *regardless of the outcome*.[5]

Effort moralization is woven through the lives of the Unfulfilled Achievers striving to be seen as both competent and virtuous at work. This is one of many ways that we tie productivity to character. What contributes to our success wound is not the very act of going above and beyond or putting in long hours when we so choose. Rather, it's what our culture makes it mean: You're a good person if you take on more.

These days, as participation in religion has declined and education has risen, work has become a substitute for the identity, purpose, and community that religion once offered. Derek Thompson calls this phenomenon *workism*, a term coined in his 2019 piece in *The Atlantic*. He defines workism as "the belief that work is not only necessary to economic production, but also the centerpiece of one's identity and life's purpose; and the belief that any policy to promote human welfare must always encourage more work."[6]

Our dissatisfaction lives in the mismatch between the promises of workism and the realities of modern work. I hear women, particularly in the Seeker archetype, yearning to find their "purpose," plotting a career path as if it were a map to their freedom and transcendence. What they are actually seeking is clarity. They want to know who they are, where they are going, and why it matters. Work offers a lot—structure, benefits, esteem, dignity, a salary—but it cannot answer these most pressing and personal questions.

Hard work is also a sign of wealth and status. In his book *The Meritocracy Trap*, Daniel Markovits writes, "Asking how long people have studied and how hard they work reveals not how poor they are but how rich."[7] Busyness is now an indication of economic opportunity. As a business owner, when people ask me how I am, the correct reply is "I'm busy," which would convey that there's an abundance of opportunities. The language of my response also links my identity ("I am") to my productivity (busy, booked, productive), subtly reinforcing my goodness and value in capitalistic terms.

If busyness is treated like a virtue, then rest starts to feel like a vice. In a blog post, activist and author of *Rest Is Resistance: A Manifesto* Tricia Hersey explains, "Capitalism was created on plantations during chattel slavery and is the same system that is driving the entire globe to exhaustion and a deep disconnection with our bodies and minds today. We are no longer divine human beings in this system and instead machines."[8] We exist within a system that dehumanizes us. We internalize our own dehumanization by tying our personal value to our productivity.

What happens when we are forced to be "unproductive" by modern standards? I've worked with women who temporarily step off the professional ladder for maternity leave and mental health leave, or take a career pause to care for their children. Switching roles from capital-producing to caregiving or healing can cause an unexpected shift in personal identity. My client Mei, head of product at a health-tech company, summed it up well: "The only reason I didn't have a total meltdown on maternity leave was because I knew how hard I worked to deserve this benefit. And I also knew how hard I was going to work when I returned. Without that knowledge, I wouldn't have been able to switch from nursing chair, to couch, to bed all day long without questioning my entire existence."

Mei isn't alone in propping her identity against her work, only to watch it collapse when the scaffolding is gone.

Americans tend to place greater importance on jobs that provide high income and opportunities for advancement.[9] Yet caregivers also generate monumental economic value. According to a report by AARP, family caregivers provide $600 billion in unpaid care in the United States.[10] Despite this, caregiving is treated as invisible, undervalued labor rather than essential economic work. It is an example of how the further away one gets from capitalist values in their work, the less social standing they enjoy.

Hard work builds both our self-esteem and the world's most groundbreaking innovations. In no way am I advocating against effort. It's necessary, it's noble, and it can be deeply fulfilling. The distinction I want to make is this: Hard work becomes a problem when it's driven by fear, shame, or a belief that our worth is measured by our output. That's when it morphs into effort moralization, the idea that your goodness, your value, your very humanity is earned by how productive you are. That's not work. That's worship.

There are periods throughout our careers where it is entirely necessary and gratifying to go above and beyond in order to get ahead, to put in long hours to finish a deal, and to devote all of one's energy and brainpower to get a project over the line. The book you have in your hands now was written mostly between the hours of 5 a.m. and 10 a.m. I woke up early to get in some good writing hours before a full day of client meetings. I was pregnant at the time and turned down invitations to dinners or a friend's comedy show so I could wake up well rested to write. I spent Sunday mornings doing administrative tasks that had piled up. Some people suggested I slow down, but I knew this message mattered. I wanted to give it everything I had before my son came. That wasn't pressure, it was purpose. I chose that hustle. I was proud of it. That's the beauty of hard work—it shows us what we're made of.

So the question isn't whether we should work hard. It's why. Are you working from a desire to collaborate, contribute, create, or crack a problem? Or just trying to prove you deserve to exist? In other words, is your hard work coming from your success wound or your wholeness? That's a central question we will continue to evaluate.

The Gender Pay Gap and the Maternal Wall

Despite important advances, there are signals that our culture continues to undervalue the work of women. It's no wonder we learn to question ourselves in a culture that does the same. First and foremost, this is evident in the gender pay gap, which is a measurement of the difference in earnings between men and women. Despite a greater awareness around the issue, the gender gap in pay has remained relatively stable in the United States over the past twenty years. In 2024, women earned an average of 85 percent of what men earned, according to a Pew Research Center analysis of median hourly earnings of both full- and part-time workers.[11] These results are similar to where the pay gap stood in 2003, when women earned 81 percent as much as men. In 2022, Black and Hispanic women experienced the largest pay gap, with Black women earning 70 cents to every white, non-Hispanic dollar, even with a graduate degree.[12]

There's also an economic penalty to being a working mother. There is no government-subsidized child care in the United States, unlike other countries, such as Canada, Australia, and Sweden. While flexible work is on the rise in some companies, maternal and gender discrimination remain. When my client Mei returned to work after her maternity leave, she discovered that two major product areas had been permanently transferred to another team member, leaving her with less prestigious products in her remit and a lower likelihood of getting her bonus. Her boss explained that these products had to go to someone who was going to give 110 percent of their focus and time. "They assumed that I wasn't going to be as dedicated to my work now that I was a mother," Mei said.

Mei's experience is indicative of the maternal wall, the barrier to advancement working mothers hit after having their first child. Research has shown that even women who *might* become pregnant also fall victim to the "maybe baby effect," a reluctance to award a woman of childbearing age promotions or opportunities because she might be out on maternity leave soon.[13]

Many working mothers are forced to prove that motherhood won't get in the way of their career by producing at an even higher level or working the same hours they had before maternity leave. When I asked Mei how this pressure affected her day-to-day, she replied, "It's exhausting to live with the constant worry that if I don't overdeliver, then they might think I'm slacking." While eliminating biases like the maternal wall are impossible to do alone, Mei was able to find new ways to get around it. She was intentional about what she worked on and how she worked, in a way that centered both her work and her impact (more on this in Chapters 6 and 7).

In an attempt to curb the epidemic of working mothers leaving the workplace, Sheryl Sandberg famously wrote her book (and motto) *Lean In*. Sandberg insisted women could make it in corporations through relentless work and unflinching personal responsibility. But Sandberg overlooked structural bias in suggesting these two factors were enough for a woman to succeed professionally. While personal agency is an important factor in career advancement, it makes women feel like failures if they can't make it work. Additionally, it supposes a binary option of being either a working mother or a stay-at-home mother, when in fact some women may step off the corporate ladder for a time, maybe have a side business or do part-time work, and choose to return to a company later. Years later, Michelle Obama correctly observed, "It's not always enough to lean in, because that shit doesn't work all the time."

Women without kids are in a different bind. Talia is the only woman of her seniority without children. "All the shit rolls downhill to me," she explained. "If someone can't meet a deadline because of school drop-off, I'm expected to pick up the slack. I've worked Christmas Day, Easter Sunday, and all the hours where my colleagues are off for bath time. From my vantage point, working parents are granted more concessions than single, childless people." Talia's perspective is illustrative of the plight of the working woman without children. Talia sought out coaching to find a new way of working that didn't result in burnout and people pleasing. "The fact that I *can* work all the time doesn't mean that I should. And I'm saying that just as much to myself as I am to the world."

In an attempt to keep up in a sick culture, women get physically sick. In the intake survey responses I've received from over two thousand working women seeking coaching, 78 percent of them stated that they've had physical ailments arising from a litany of workplace stressors. In my own career, I was plagued with chronic sinus infections that would arise like clockwork whenever I pushed past my capacity, sprinting toward a deadline for longer than a few months. In his book *The Myth of Normal: Trauma, Illness, and Healing in a Toxic Culture*, Dr. Gabor Maté argues that women's chronic illness can arise from social causes. Maté explains how rising rates of chronic illness, addiction, and mental health issues are a result of inequality and poverty, disproportionately affecting women and underrepresented and under-resourced communities. "Women often serve as the emotional glue—the connective tissue, if you like—that keeps nuclear and extended families and communities together. In our ailing culture, it is no coincidence they suffer far more than men do from diseases of actual connective tissue, among which lupus, rheumatoid arthritis, scleroderma, fibromyalgia, and their multiple relatives are variants. These conditions, as most chronic maladies do, reflect social dynamics, not simply individual physiology gone rogue."[14]

While it's shocking to see the effects that the systematic devaluing of women in society has on our physical health, perhaps it's not surprising. Patriarchy and capitalism are an enormous weight on the psychology and physiology of women in the workplace and beyond. The result? Women who are stuck in scarcity, competition, and working overtime to prove they can hack it. Toxic corporate cultures are often characterized by this scarcity and competition that erodes our esteem and belonging.

Toxic Workplace Cultures

My team at Google had a morale problem, so the managers called a team meeting to discuss the dynamics of our team culture. We sat around a brightly lit conference table and looked at each other apprehensively. I don't remember the full agenda, but I do remember there being a supposed open floor for people to voice their concerns.

A woman on my team raised her hand and shared that she'd observed a toxic culture on our team. When our director pushed my colleague to define what she meant by "toxic culture," it was hard for her to quantify. I squirmed with discomfort as my teammate tried to name something I felt too, but couldn't quite articulate. It was as if the culture had become so normalized we couldn't express its abnormality.

I wish I had had the language that's available now to describe what I experienced. In an attempt to bring observable behavior to what can be a nebulous phenomenon, a 2022 study from MIT Sloan characterized toxic culture with five attributes: lack of inclusion (cultures that are characterized by words like *cliquey*, *clubby*, *in-crowd* that indicate some employees are excluded either because of their identity markers or without specifying why), unethical behavior, cutthroat competition, bullying, and disrespect. These attributes corrode trust, deplete morale, and are the largest predictor of attrition.[15]

Women have been calling out toxic workplaces for decades. In the 1990s, Anita Hill brought forward workplace sexual harassment allegations against Clarence Thomas, then a Supreme Court justice nominee. These hearings brought national attention to the widespread reality of workplace harassment and the painful truth that women were neither believed nor protected. In 2017, the #MeToo movement, founded by American activist Tarana Burke, pulled back the curtain even further on exposing how deeply rooted this culture remains in the workplace. In 2021, employees at gaming company Activision Blizzard staged a walkout to protest what they described as a "frat boy workplace culture," where rape jokes were made openly and women were paid less than men. Despite increased awareness and mandatory trainings, McKinsey & Company's 2024 *Women in the Workplace* study reported that sexual harassment remains just as prevalent today, even after the #MeToo movement.[16]

Back at the "open floor" discussion, my director turned to the rest of the room. "Does anyone else think we have a culture problem here?" No one else raised their hand. I glanced down at mine, half expecting it to move on its own, but it stayed still. As quickly as I had recognized what my colleague was talking about, my mind began to rationalize that maybe we didn't have one. Was there a culture problem if I couldn't prove it? Or was it all in my head? Could a company that offered benefits like egg freezing and generous maternity leave still harbor a culture problem? And what would happen if I raised my hand and spoke up? As I mentally debated myself, I stayed silent along with the other people on the team, and the meeting moved on.

On my walk home, I thought back to this meeting. I realized I contributed to this culture, too. I would repeat tropes like "no pain, no gain" as I competed to hit a revenue target that went up-and-to-the-right by 20 percent quarter after quarter after quarter. I was "moving fast and breaking things," attending all the company-sponsored happy hours and concerts where only select people were invited, all for the approval of—and the benefit of—a corporate culture that profited from my ambition. I desperately needed to belong. My success wound and the toxic culture reinforced each other. I was complicit in the culture because I didn't see another way to be.

Today, many of my coaching clients talk about the guilt they carry from feeling like they have to leave their humanity at the door when they walk into work. They say they are one version of themselves in their personal lives, and work brings out a different side of them—colder, more reserved, less confident. The success wound was working within you before you got to the workplace. And yet the culture of the workplace likely manipulated and exacerbated your insecurities to its own advantage.

It's no wonder that women question their deservingness and credibility after working in such environments. More often, I see my clients assume that there's something wrong with *them*, rather than with the culture they're navigating. They think, *I can't keep up, I don't have what it takes. If I'm not listened to, then I need to speak up more.* This is actually an intended consequence of toxic workplaces: to keep employees questioning their standing so that they will work harder to keep it.

What About Imposter Syndrome?

My client Talia thought her people pleasing and empty-cup feeling were rooted in imposter syndrome—a persistent belief that she was not as capable or smart as others believed her to be. That she didn't deserve her "Director" title and that if she didn't maintain good standing and performance, others would see this. Was this the same thing as the success wound? Not quite.

The success wound and imposter syndrome are related but distinct. The former is the socialized habit of pinning our worthiness to what we achieve and produce, and the latter is the resulting feeling of self-doubt. Imposter syndrome would disappear if we believed deeply in our inherent worth.

Imposter phenomenon was first named by psychologists Suzanne Imes and Pauline Rose Clance as an observation among women students and other marginalized groups in college settings. These individuals experience pervasive feelings of self-doubt and fear of being exposed as a fraud in their work, despite verifiable and objective evidence of their success.[17] Fifty-five percent of women report that they have felt inadequate at their job at least once or twice in the last week, and young men report feeling this way 46 percent of the time.[18]

And yet what has traditionally been called imposter syndrome places the sickness on the individual, not on the culture. In their viral article published in *Harvard Business Review*, authors Ruchika Tulshyan and Jodi-Ann Burey aptly point out, "Imposter syndrome puts the blame on individuals, without accounting for the historical and cultural contexts that are foundational to how it manifests in both women of color and white women. Imposter syndrome directs our view toward fixing women at work instead of fixing the places where women work."[19]

The same argument could be made for the terminology of the success wound. A few clients rightfully insist they are not broken or wounded. I agree. *They* are not those things. Yet a part of them has been hurt by a pervasive belief system and culture that teaches them to value what they do over who they are. The system is wounded, and a part of our psyche is in turn hurt by the system. We are not the source of the brokenness. However, the consequences of living and working from a perceived deficiency are the same: burnout, anxiety, and even chronic pain.

What About Perfectionism?

Almost all Unfulfilled Achievers struggle with perfectionism—the habit of placing unrealistically high standards on oneself, and measuring one's self-worth against the achievement or, more likely, failure to reach this standard. When we believe that our lovability and belonging depends on what we produce, it's an understandable impulse to want to control every deliverable, every project, every piece of code, every career decision, and how we come across.

Each type of Unfulfilled Achiever pursues perfection slightly differently. Grinders place a high standard on their productivity, as they believe that the more they can get done, the more perfect they will seem. Hiders want to be perfect in their choices. Their fear of making the wrong choice or being judged as unsuccessful keeps them from moving forward in their lives. Seekers similarly idolize the perfect career, the ideal opportunity, or the validation of a promotion, hoping that the perceived perfection of their career will reflect on them. Pleasers, on the other hand, want to be perfect in their interactions, never being too demanding, too mean, overbearing, or rocking the boat; they seek control in being liked. Work Hard, Play Hards define perfection as their ability to be everything to everyone and do everything flawlessly, from how they lead a meeting, to how they vacation, to how they reorganize their homes.

Thus perfectionism is a symptom of the success wound. Heal your success wound and the sting of perfectionism lessens with it.

THE CONSEQUENCES OF THE SUCCESS WOUND

You don't have to look far to see the mental and physical impact of the success wound within working women. In fact, you may be reading this book currently suffering from burnout or having been through periods of depression or chronic pain. By now, you might have a hunch that it's related to your relationship to work. Let's look at the studies and data to validate that hunch for you.

Burnout

It will not come as a surprise to hear that of the thousands of Unfulfilled Achievers I've worked with, 80 percent of them experience burnout. It's exhausting to live and work in a constant state of fight, flight, freeze, or fawn that comes from tying your value to your professional outcomes. Burnout has three dimensions: energy depletion or exhaustion, increased mental distance from one's job (e.g., disillusionment, absenteeism, low engagement), and reduced professional efficacy.[20] These can all lead to lack of motivation and a loss of meaning or purpose at work.

Common beliefs indicative of the success wound are: "I have so much to do and I'll never catch up" and "I'm not doing enough." The natural response to feeling behind is to work even harder to get ahead. Grinders and Work Hard, Play Hards are particularly susceptible to this trap. Working long hours is one of many other factors that lead to burnout. Office politics can be incredibly draining for an Unfulfilled Achiever, particularly Pleasers whose value comes from being liked and staying in good standing.

The double bind facing working mothers contributes massively to the burnout gap that exists across gender lines. Women are more likely than men to feel burned out at work than men (34 percent vs. 26 percent).[21] What's more, this gap has more than doubled since 2019 and disproportionately affects women in non-leadership positions. External factors like the gender pay gap and maternal wall bias contribute to burnout in addition to how the success wound operates within us.

Anxiety and Depression

Unfulfilled Achievers tend to have incredibly high standards for themselves and others. These standards aren't the entirety of the problem; it's also the suffering that arises when they fail to meet them. To them, failing can induce feelings of dread, panic, shame, and complete overwhelm.

High achievers suffer disproportionately from depression.[22] It makes sense; unrelenting standards and self-criticism contribute to feelings of hopelessness and emotional exhaustion. It's easy to blame a toxic workplace culture, a bad manager, or office politics, which can indeed contribute to poor mental health outcomes. But it's also our internalized success wounds that quietly chip away at our mental health.

I've been invited to speak at corporations about the impact of the success wound on organizations. But there's always one question that's in the back of everyone's mind: Don't companies *want* their employees to have a success wound? Doesn't that negative pressure keep people striving and producing more? Yes and no. High achievers are 400 percent more profitable than other employees for corporations, but to a point.[23] Productivity lost to burnout, depression, and anxiety costs the global economy $1 trillion per year.[24] It's easy to accept anxiety as a necessary part of getting ahead or being successful. Some anxiety can be helpful for performance.[25] But the type of unrelenting anxiety that plagues most Unfulfilled Achievers inhibits the full spectrum of their skills and strengths. In this way, employees that operate from their success wound are more of a drag on the corporate system than an asset.

For CEOs, their rate of anxiety and depression is estimated to be double the national average, ranging from 20 percent to as high as 50 percent.[26] This is a striking dichotomy between our reverence for the title of CEO, and the reality of its burden. My client Joy is the CEO of an insurance brokerage a few hours outside San Antonio. She described the unrelenting pressure this way: "I'm responsible for thousands of people's livelihoods. It's overwhelming and keeps me up at night." Joy had been treated for anxiety and depression for years. Therapy and medication helped. In our introductory call, she acknowledged how her working patterns contribute to this panic: "I know that I need to hold my work differently. Right now I'm gripping it tight like a fish on a line. If I want to actually enjoy this position and the final years of my career, I'm going to need to change how I work." I asked Joy how she would characterize her ways of working. "Compulsive and addictive," she replied.

Workaholism and Addiction

We are only as free as our dependencies. A cycle of suffering emerges when we become dependent upon work or other substances to relieve the success wound's pain. And yes, work itself can become an addiction—over the years, many of my clients have described their relationship with work this way. I remember my first call with Joy, who described work as both her source of relief and her source of suffering. "I could feel insane all weekend—anxious about my kids, worried about my future—but when I open my laptop, there's a relief that comes at once." For Joy, work offered a rare sense of control. "I can organize a spreadsheet, I can perfect a presentation to the board and get good feedback. At work, there are clear rules and I can play by them well," she explained.

Joy once described work as her happy place. "It's not work because I love doing it," she said. There's nothing to pathologize about loving your work and finding a vocation that's a passion and an interest for you. For many of my clients, that's their professional goal. The workaholism isn't found in the long hours or in the work itself, but in the impact these working habits have on your health and relationships.

Joy used work to self-soothe, which in turn stole from other areas of her life. Her marriage was suffering because her best energy went into work. Her kids complained that she was always on her phone. She used work as an excuse to avoid any potential social discomfort, like attending her college reunion even though her friends would be there.

Eventually, her family became more and more concerned. Her team started to resent the emails she sent at all hours of the night. Joy could recognize that work was causing more problems for her than solving them. But she couldn't stop. Sometimes she rationalized her compulsive work habits as necessary to provide for her family or to get the business through a stressful period. But deep down, Joy started questioning if it was all worth it.

Ultimately, the choice to examine your working patterns—or to label them as workaholism—is yours. When considering whether your relationship to work is compulsive or addictive, Dr. Maté offers this definition: "Any behavior that gives temporary relief, temporary pleasure, but in the long term causes harm, has some negative consequences, and you cannot stop the behavior despite the negative consequences."[27] When I shared this definition with Joy, she agreed that her work compulsions fit this description. Once Joy was able to take steps to address her unconscious pain of unworthiness (outlined in Chapter 5) and find a new way of working (outlined in Chapter 7), her workaholism abated significantly.

In addition to workaholism, we all have ways of relieving the pressure and turning the heat down to varying degrees. For many of my peers it was booking vacations. They enjoy fantasizing about the meals, the beach, and the relief they would feel once on the plane. The image of the vacation served as an escape from their unpleasant reality. For others, it's distracting with email, social media, online shopping, or Bravo TV. A certain amount of escapism is beneficial and healthy. But it veers into unhealthy territory when indulging becomes a way we avoid addressing the larger issues in our lives or when we overdo it.

For me, partying became both my pressure valve and my purpose, giving me something to work hard *for*. It was a pressure valve I could pull to release the steam that had built up inside me all week. A beer at happy hour seemed like the only way to quiet my work anxieties. Eventually my drinking became something I *had* to do rather than something I *chose* to do for fun. The consequences of my binge drinking piled up: stomach issues, insomnia, hurt friendships, and a dwindling savings account. But I couldn't stop. For my clients, especially those in the Work Hard, Play Hard category, they can turn to binge eating and even prescription drugs to check out from their feelings of inadequacy and pressure. It wasn't until I addressed the underlying reasons that I needed to escape that I could exit this addiction cycle.

Illness, Chronic Pain, and Physical Symptoms

It's widely accepted that the body and mind operate as a connected and integrated force.[28] Our thoughts and emotions affect our behavior, which can in turn affect our physical health. When we are dependent upon our achievements to bring confidence and esteem, then our failures can threaten our sense of safety and identity. In one of our first conversations, my client Talia, the media executive, told me, "My body bears the brunt of my stress." When big presentations or deadlines would approach, the panic of not delivering to her high expectations affected her sleep and her immune system. She was constantly fending off sinus infections, bouts of tonsillitis, and joint pain.

Talia also experienced chronic back pain for years, yet MRIs and scans never showed a point of injury. She used some homeopathic remedies from her childhood, which helped for a short period but didn't deliver sustainable relief. During our sessions she would complain of flare-ups, especially during times of extreme stress at work.

Talia's doctor pointed her to tension myositis syndrome (TMS), a field of study for chronic back pain discovered by Dr. John Sarno. The theory of tension myositis syndrome is that your mind creates pain symptoms in the back to distract from repressed emotional pain. In Talia's case, her body was carrying the weight of unprocessed shame and unworthiness. This diagnosis coincided with Talia working to strengthen her connection with her True Self and work from her wholeness. She came into our session one day with news that shocked me. "My chronic back pain has been gone for a month. This is the longest period of remission I've ever had." We were both delighted, as was her doctor. In working to address the emotional manifestations of her success wound, the physical pain cleared with it.

A NEW VISION FOR SUCCESS: THE IMPERATIVE OF HEALING

Most people don't want to question the enduring notions of success that have been handed to them by their culture. It's easier to believe in an ideal of success that's socially acceptable, even if it winds up, paradoxically, curtailing your satisfaction and diminishing your power.

But you are different. You are an achiever; you see an inspiring vision for yourself and others and have the drive to make it a reality.

Your power is dynamic, and your momentum is inevitable. When you see something you want, nothing gets in your way. There's absolutely nothing to pathologize about that. Our shared work is to help you choose to belong to yourself more than you belong to an outdated definition of success, one that keeps you stuck, striving, and searching for significance in all the wrong places. You deserve more than the confining existence that burnout and anxiety bring. You deserve to rest in your inherent goodness and to feel the truth of who you are in every cell of your body.

Healing your success wound is not just personal, it's cultural. When you begin to heal, you help heal the sick systems around us. This work starts with you, but it ripples outward. The first step in healing any wound is to get a proper diagnosis. Now that you understand the roots of your success wound, from childhood through today, it's time to explore how it shows up in your working life by identifying your primary Unfulfilled Achiever archetype.

QUIZ

What Is Your Unfulfilled Achiever Type?

What kind of Unfulfilled Achiever are you? These five types are distilled from the behavioral patterns commonly seen in high-achieving women driven by their success wound. While you may identify strongly with one dominant Unfulfilled Achiever type, it's likely that you embody multiple types—or different aspects of them—that show up in various contexts or at different stages of your career. I don't break out "the Perfectionist" or "the Inner Critic" into their own categories because all these types are informed by perfectionism, self-criticism, self-doubt, and judgment. As you move through the next chapter, I encourage you to read about each type. They often show up within us to varying degrees, and recognizing their influence is a powerful part of the healing process.

You can also find a digital version of this quiz at brooketaylorcoaching.com/quiz.

1. **Your boss calls you in and gives you some good feedback! How do you feel?**
    a. Happy, but the feeling doesn't last long. You get back to work; still so much to get done!
    b. Not surprised because you've been doing this type of role and work for a while. You know what you're doing.
    c. You're relieved and slightly surprised because you've been checked out recently.
    d. Elated. You can't get enough good praise and feedback.
    e. You're pumped and use the feedback as an excuse to celebrate with your favorite treat or experience.

2. **Which statement sounds most like you?**
    a. You're regularly burned out or exhausted from overworking and the constant need to be productive.
    b. You tend to stay in your comfort zone, doing well at the level you're at, but deep down know you're meant for more.
    c. Each job you're in gets boring after a while and you're often wondering if this career is really "it."
    d. You put the needs of your boss, colleagues, and clients over your own.
    e. You work hard during the week and need to release the pressure at night and on the weekends.

3. **What's one toxic habit you wish you could stop?**
   a. Working to the point of burnout and overwhelm.
   b. Avoiding or procrastinating tasks that feel unfamiliar or risky.
   c. Comparing yourself with others and saying things like, "I wish I had their career."
   d. Obsessing over conversations with your boss or coworkers—replaying what you said.
   e. Taking the edge off with food, alcohol, or other substances that make you feel unhealthy.

4. **Which thought most frequently crosses your mind at work?**
   a. "If I'm not the best, what's the point?"
   b. "I want more for my career, but I'm afraid to fail or put myself out there."
   c. "What am I even doing with my life?"
   d. "What do they think of me?"
   e. "This week is nonstop—meetings, social events, everything. I'll rest all weekend and bounce back."

5. Which work pattern feels most familiar?

a. You believe hard work always pays off and you grind to get to the next level.

b. You kill it at your role, but you rarely take bold risks.

c. You often feel lost, unsure if you are on the right career path.

d. You're only as good as your last piece of feedback from a manager or colleague.

e. You tend to work and live in extremes—you're either booked and busy or recovering from a stressful week.

6. You're offered a new, challenging job. You're flattered, but how do you feel the next day?

a. You're ready, but a small voice asks, "Will this run me into the ground?"

b. You hesitate. It feels risky leaving the safety of a role you know.

c. You're excited, maybe this is *finally* the career path you've been looking for forever.

d. You're nervous—worried what your boss will think if you resign. You don't want to let anyone down.

e. You're in if it is a cool company with visibility and new opportunities.

7. **According to your colleagues, you are…**

    a. The "Get Shit Done" Person: You will get it done well and fast.

    b. The Expert: You've killed it at one thing for a while and are a master at your craft.

    c. The Jack of All Trades: You've had a lot of different jobs and experiences you can leverage.

    d. Mrs. Reliable: You'll drop everything to help a new colleague, pick up the slack, or plan an office event if asked.

    e. The Life of the Office: You infuse everything with an intensity that makes work both fun and successful.

8. **What is your biggest fear?**

    a. Falling behind or stagnating.

    b. Staying stuck in your same job or at the same level forever.

    c. Never discovering your purpose or dream career.

    d. Disappointing people—or being misunderstood.

    e. Regretting not doing and seeing everything you want to see.

If you got mostly A's, you are The Grinder

If you got mostly B's, you are The Hider

If you got mostly C's, you are The Seeker

If you got mostly D's, you are The Pleaser

If you got mostly E's, you are The Work Hard, Play Hard

CHAPTER 2

THE FIVE TYPES OF UNFULFILLED ACHIEVERS

How the Success Wound Manifests in Your Career

Mei was reeling. She had just been promoted to head of product at a health-tech company in San Francisco. She was the only woman in a senior leadership position and the only person of color. Six months in, something happened she never saw coming: She received a below-average performance rating. Her team complained about micromanagement and a complete lack of work-life balance.

"I excel at execution," Mei explained to me in our first coaching session on Zoom. "I have this ability to focus and get shit done. As a software engineer, this was my competitive edge and why I got promoted." But the new role demanded a different skill set: managing, leading, and setting a product strategy. She knew how to lead teams—she'd done it before in her career as a software engineering manager. But this time, the stakes felt impossibly high. Her boss, the chief product officer, said if this next product launch didn't go smoother than the last, they might need to find a new role for her.

Deep down, Mei believed that failing meant she was a failure—a core belief rooted in her success wound. She conceded she did micromanage—she couldn't trust her team enough to relinquish control. She explained, "No one can do it as well or as fast as I can. When they deliver suboptimal work, it's exhausting to coach them through the fixes. I can't risk any mistakes. With tight deadlines, I'd rather just fix it myself." Delegating felt like gambling, and she never gambled. She ran on spreadsheets and adrenaline.

Mei leaned on her inner Grinder, plowing through work with sheer will, the same strategy that had once helped her succeed as the only Korean American student in a small private school in San Francisco. But this strategy no longer worked in her career; instead, it robbed her of critical leadership skills, the respect of her team, and the ability to flourish in the role she had coveted. The Grinder part of her was so dominant that it eclipsed her ability to collaborate and lead.

Such is the paradox of the Unfulfilled Achiever: The well-intentioned strategies that were once used to get ahead, to win others over, and to achieve are often the very things keeping you from the next level of success and from fulfillment that lasts longer than a few days. Eventually, the very strategies that helped you rise begin to hold you back.

These behaviors are *attempting* to protect you from failure, to prevent you from being judged as a fraud, or to stop you from falling behind. These beliefs arise from a fear of not being enough just as you are. Through this lens, we can have compassion for the Unfulfilled Achiever parts of us that are attempting to keep us moving forward.

Let me start a new paragraph so I can say this as emphatically as possible: Each of these Unfulfilled Achiever types you'll read about in this chapter carries real strengths. Not flaws to fix, but traits to recognize, honor, and harness. There's nothing wrong with working hard, with caring deeply, with wanting more, or striving to become your best self. Any behavior can be a hindrance or an asset depending upon how it's used and where it's coming *from*—a place of wounding, or a place of wholeness. You just haven't learned how to maximize the strengths and minimize the suffering.

Most of us hold all these types inside us. One or two primary types usually rise to the surface, shaped by your industry, the stage of your career, or your natural strengths. For example, perhaps you exhibited Work Hard, Play Hard tendencies early on in your career before a mortgage and family, which then brought out your Hider who is afraid to risk financial insecurity. Or maybe you rely on your Grinder and Pleaser equally when you onboard into a new company. These types aren't fixed. You might have exhibited all these types at different times in your career—maybe even all of them in a single day.

As you read through these five types, remember that we aren't here to pathologize your work ethic or point to the flaws in your being. Shame is an ineffective motivator for change. Instead, read the rest of this book starting from this essential premise:

Everything you are is good. Any other belief that suggests you are not good enough is just FEAR—False Evidence Appearing Real.

The quickest way to access your True Self is through curiosity; being curious means to hold something lightly and say, "Hmm, that's interesting. I wonder how this got here?" So let's tap into your curiosity and explore the five types of Unfulfilled Achievers.

THE GRINDER

As a Grinder, you believe the longer and harder you work, the better off you will be. You are a manager's dream, relentlessly tackling your to-do list, hitting deadlines, and delivering results, but all the gold stars you get can come at the expense of your mental and physical health. You're tired. Exhausted. Depleted. You often come last on your never-ending priority list, causing bitterness and burnout.

Grinders are motivated by being valued for their productivity. In this way, most achievers have at least some Grinder tendencies. They love being called the "get shit done" person or being referred to as "a secret weapon" by their manager. Focused on both quality and quantity, a Grinder's work ethic is a tremendous asset to teams as they are given more and more responsibility. But that drive, which was once esteem-building, turns soul-crushing when it's fueled by a sense of lack—a need for the Grinder to prove themselves, or else.

Mei was no exception. She credited her work ethic with both her rise and her unraveling. She came to me in a state of severe burnout and at a loss after her performance review. How did she get here?

At forty-one, this title was a big step up in her career that she had worked toward for years. She was both motivated by the challenge and equally terrified of squandering the opportunity by dropping a ball or appearing incompetent.

She received her promotion in February 2020, right before San Francisco went into a COVID lockdown. "During the pandemic, all I did was work," Mei recounted. "At first, I loved it. I had no commute and no guilt about missing birthday parties or trips. My husband quit his job to take care of our twin boys, which we could now do financially on my higher salary. I disappeared into work and no one questioned it. I could control everything and make sure I never missed something. The control gave me some confidence that I could succeed in this senior role."

A Grinder's work ethic is not only a great asset; it is also rewarded. But it is this very reputation that can prevent a Grinder from developing other skills like delegating and inspiring their team, because they rely on being a productivity machine. This is the Grinder trap: believing your entire value lies in your ability to grind.

When I asked Mei to share what her relationship with achievement and success looked like growing up, she replied that she was practically born feeling behind. "Everything seemed to come so naturally to my older brother and we were constantly compared. There was a narrative in my family that academics came harder for me so I needed to work twice as hard for half the results." She was raised with the belief that achievement wasn't optional; it was survival. Her parents had sacrificed everything for the chance at a better life, and that legacy lived inside her like a quiet contract: *You don't get to rest. You don't get to fail.* Her Korean mother had immigrated to California and had taught herself English. She got a job as a school administrator and created a life for herself. Work ethic was cultural, generational, and deeply tied to familial duty. The unspoken understanding was that her worth was measured by how hard she worked, how much she produced, and how little she complained.

Mei took this belief from her home in San Francisco, to an undergrad and graduate degree in computer science, and into her first job back in the Bay Area. Along the way, she believed she needed to work much harder than her peers to keep up. The lie that she wasn't naturally gifted took root, growing into low self-esteem that bled into every area of her life too, like keeping her social circle small and working out to punish her body.

For some Grinders, like Mei, growing up they internalized that they weren't naturally as smart, athletic, or gifted as everyone else. As a result, they tried to make up for it with an incredible work ethic, believing hard work could bridge the gap between their supposedly deficient capabilities and success.

Other Grinders had the opposite experience as children. School came easily to them. They grew dependent upon the label of being "naturally gifted" or "top of the class" because they saw the attention, praise, and approval from their parents or teachers for their striving and achievements. It's no wonder they worked harder and longer—chasing the praise that had once felt like love.

Mei had a lifelong dream to attend university, so a scholarship was a necessity. On top of being a great student, she was an elite soccer player. "My future was on my shoulders. Whether I qualified for the varsity soccer team or failed. Whether I went to university or not. On the one hand, it was empowering to feel so in control of my life from a young age. But mostly I remember feeling so alone, like it was me against the world." Mei learned to push through discomfort: She pushed her body to its limits on the soccer field, pushed down the loneliness of being seventeen and filing scholarship papers, and later pushed aside her desire to be a computer science teacher when her parents encouraged her to go into business.

Mei's Grinder, in turn, pushed her to her limit. Her anxiety became overwhelming and her insomnia became debilitating. Her husband was worried for her health. Her breaking point came in the form of the low performance review and the feedback that she needed to find a new way to lead her team or else they'd have to find a different role for her. She was dejected, demoralized, and completely unsure how she could lead and work in a more sustainable manner.

During one of our earlier sessions, Mei described herself in a poignant way. She began, "I let my four-year-old boys watch *Shark Week* on Discover. I heard about a type of shark that has to always be swimming to survive. I mean, how exhausting. But I am that shark! I can't stop swimming and I am so tired of it."

I could only imagine just how tired she was. Mei and I started working together after years of pushing through the unimaginable: multiple workplace bullying claims, four promotions, and endless toxic managers. "I don't know any other way to work other than full throttle or falling apart," she said, tears catching in her throat. My heart broke for Mei. I could see the young girl still swimming, resourceful, relentless, without a soft place to rest.

The key to freedom and fulfillment for the Grinder is to install a third and fourth gear of operating so they don't have to work at full throttle. Learning how to turn on their turbo work ethic when required, and learning how to focus on fewer, higher-impact priorities at other times. This new behavior is only possible from a shift in their perceived value originating from their being, not their doing. When Grinders channel their ambition toward the direction of their True Self, not their success wound, that's when freedom begins.

GRINDER CHEAT SHEET

Motivation:

Belief that constant effort and hard work will eventually lead to the validation and love they seek.

They love when you call them:

- The best
- The "get shit done" person
- Reliable

The gifts:

- Work ethic
- Great team players
- Exceptional individual contributors

The shadow:

- Judgmental of themselves and others
- Difficulty shifting from doing the work to leading the work
- Forever unsatisfied: Never feel like enough despite all the success on paper
- Black-and-white thinking: *If I work hard at it, the results should come.*

THE HIDER

It's hard to spot a Hider in the wild because they, well, hide in plain sight. They are experts in their field, kill it at what they do, and appear remarkably put together. On the surface, they're seen as loyal, capable, and committed, the kind of steady hand any team wants. Their ambition runs just as deep, but it's buried under fear: of failure, rejection, or falling into financial insecurity. Underneath it all, they tend to cling to their comfort zone and fear leaving it more than they desire change.

One of these Hiders was Sutton, the woman whom I met in the Financial District of New York who described her success wound as an "empty cup." Her friends saw the brave woman who had left her small town in rural Louisiana and parlayed a temp job at a large investment bank into a full-time role. She had worked her way up to vice president. Her career was "good on paper," and that became both her armor and her trap. Sutton knew a deeper truth about herself—one that she was hiding.

For the last ten years she'd lived in the same modest but tasteful one-bedroom apartment overlooking the Charles River in Boston. She often traveled between Boston and New York for business, so half our sessions were in person in New York, and the other half were online. In a virtual coaching session, she pulled at the collar of her black wool turtleneck that accentuated the white blond of her hair as she shared: "I am stuck in this place where everything is 'good enough' that I'm so scared to make a leap and mess it all up. I want to leave finance but it pays so well. I have glimmers of hope that I can find a career that pays me well and I'm happy with, but what if I take the leap and fall? I don't have a financial safety net—no partner, no family money. I've thought about moving into a more updated apartment but hold off in case I finally switch jobs and my salary goes down. The fear is paralyzing, like living in a six-foot prison I built myself." Sutton knew there was more for her but couldn't get out of her own way.

Hiders tend to be expert avoiders, always putting off change or discomfort, which can masquerade as responsibility. The Hider's inner voice is subtle, even convincing: *Let me just save a little more money, then I'll make the change*, or *I just had a baby, let me get my feet under me and then I'll look for the real job I want*. But the goalpost keeps moving. Months turn into years and no action is taken. They're haunted by the idea of giving it their all and still falling short.

Hiders are also optimistic and hopeful that things will get better or change—that their boss might change their tune and be the exceptional manager he has the potential to be, that the glimmers of joy they find in their work will somehow expand. But sometimes this naive optimism is actually another form of avoidance.

Hiders are motivated by certainty. As such, they fear the uncomfortable uncertainty that's required to make a career change. Sutton told me, "I feel ungrateful even thinking about leaving. My job is stable. I have benefits. I'm lucky. How can I know if it's the right decision to leave?" Racing questions flooded her mind: *What if the commute is longer and I can't make it to my favorite yoga class? What if my salary is lower and I'm forced to sacrifice my quality of life? Will I enjoy my colleagues as much in my next role? What if my boss hates me?* Hiders like Sutton ultimately land on status quo, logically convincing themselves that the devil they know is better than the devil they don't, at least for now.

They are also very dedicated and loyal to their team, boss, company, and work. The desire for change is there but often outshined by the grief of letting go: of routines, colleagues, and the career they've spent years building. This loyalty can be both genuine and a cover for their inaction.

Hiders can also have Grinder and Pleaser tendencies. Sutton had ADHD, and in her experience, her ADHD made her above average in some things and below average in others. "But I never know in which area," Sutton said, twisting a tendril of blond hair around her finger as she spoke. "I'm constantly afraid of looking dumb, especially without a traditional finance background. I prefer to operate under the radar, do good work by myself with my head down. If I'm called on or asked a question in a meeting, I freeze and my heart rate jumps. I don't speak up in meetings or raise my hand for the stretch projects that will help me progress and grow because I'm terrified of looking incompetent."

In childhood, Hiders might have had parents who were risk averse and reminded them that the world is not safe, to stay in your steady nine-to-five job, and be grateful for the paycheck. Many Hiders grew up with financial, relational, or emotional chaos, which wired their nervous systems to crave certainty above all else. Sutton's parents and grandparents had built small businesses from the ground up in Louisiana—a fishing lodge and a grocery store—working tirelessly to create stability for future generations. That legacy weighed on her. How could she abandon security to chase a dream that might not pan out? Especially when that dream didn't come with a 401(k)?

I asked Sutton about the other areas of her life and if she found herself hiding there, too. "My life feels like the movie *Groundhog Day*; it's not progressing. A day in my life seven years ago looks the same as today. I want a relationship, but I'm not dating. I've wanted to leave Boston for years, but I don't know where to go or what job I would take. I see other people passing me by, having the life I want but it seems so out of reach." Sutton had dreams and desires for a different future that started with leaving the golden handcuffs of finance, maybe starting a business like her parents did, or asking the cute guy from her gym out for lunch. She sighed. "It feels like I've traded novelty for certainty and now my life *is* certain but confining. Like it's mine but it's not mine. Does that make sense?" It made so much sense. Trade too much safety for too long, and your comfort zone becomes a cage. She was caught between the life she had built and the life she longed for.

But even those who do take a bold leap can hide. After leaving Google to start coaching full-time, my inner Hider came out in full force. I remember feeling embarrassed to tell people I was a career coach. At a friend's birthday dinner, at a long, noisy restaurant table where I knew only the birthday girl, someone asked what I did for work. My voice went high and fast: "Oh! I'm a career coach for corporate women; what do you do?" I rushed through the words in a single breath, eager to move the conversation along.

After dinner, I walked back to my car and winced as I replayed that moment in my head. *Why did I avoid talking about my job?* I loved my work. I was doing exactly what I wanted to be doing. But my inner Hider was scared to own it. I feared the secret opinions of the other girls. *Is coaching ambitious enough? Will they assume my husband is bankrolling a passion project? Will they take me more seriously if they know my corporate background? And if I don't fit into their version of success, will they still want to be friends?* My fear of judgment and inadequacy kept me hiding my accomplishments and passion for my job early on in my coaching career. That's the thing about the Hider. They often look successful, grounded, even confident. But underneath, there's a constant fear of being found out, misunderstood, or not enough.

I had compassion for Sutton's inner Hider that was trying to keep her safe. But I also knew that unless Sutton healed her success wound, she ran the risk of her Hider defining her career for years to come. Her healing wasn't about suddenly becoming fearless or quitting everything overnight. It was about learning to trust that her desires were valid. That safety didn't have to mean invisibility. And that slow, steady momentum was more than enough to change her life. I saw a flicker within Sutton that was ready for a change, and, as fate would have it, she was about to be served the perfect opportunity to rise to the occasion.

HIDER CHEAT SHEET

Motivation:

Fear of failure or rejection so they stay under the radar or in their comfort zone.

They love when you call them:

- The expert
- Invaluable
- Loyal

The gifts:

- Resourceful: They excel at doing more with less and optimizing within constraints.
- Optimistic: They are convinced the best is yet to come... even when it isn't.
- Dedicated: They are committed to their people and principles, with a clear sense of what they stand for.

The shadow:

- Avoid visibility
- Compare and despair
- Low self-esteem and self-trust
- Stay in their comfort zone
- Play it safe and small
- Internal conflict between desire for success and fear of exposure

THE SEEKER

Chances are that you have a Seeker in your life; everyone seems to know one. The person who spends their mental energy on a spectrum from confused to full-blown existential crisis, sometimes all in one day. They feel adrift, hoping a dream job will pull them aboard and rescue them from themselves. Seekers are constantly looking for the next big thing—the next job (or city or partner or dog or cleanse or guru) that is *IT* and will finally fix their anguish. Sound familiar?

Seekers are largely motivated by hope—the hope that they will someday find happiness or be saved from their racing minds. Like the Work Hard, Play Hard type, Seekers can have escapist tendencies, looking for something outside themselves to regulate an internal condition.

But don't get it twisted; if you are the Seeker archetype, you are highly intelligent and capable and can master challenges quickly. Your enthusiasm is magnetic, your conviction contagious. You are naturally curious and adept at solving problems. Which makes it even more frustrating that you can't crack this one thing: your career.

When Seekers are told, "The sky's the limit! You can do anything you set your mind to," they are equally inspired and panicked. The abundance of options and opportunities to go left or right, to stay or go, overwhelm them. Decision fatigue turns into start-up fatigue, the kind that comes from chasing a new path with complete conviction, only to realize it didn't cure the unworthiness underneath.

Self-doubt is a constant companion for the Seeker. They latch on to a new goal or vision and pursue it with renewed excitement and vigor. *This is it!* they think hopefully. Then, inevitably, the idealization starts to fall apart. Maybe they're in the job and realize the work-life balance isn't as flexible as they had hoped. Or they receive a piece of feedback that takes the wind out of their sails. Self-doubt starts to creep in: *Maybe this isn't it.* The fantasy of the vision, the next job application, and the next business plan never live up to reality. So they aim to start fresh, slowly reconstructing a new idea or vision, repeating the pattern over again.

Chelsea had spent her entire adult life searching for her calling, treating the quest for purpose like an Easter egg hunt. At thirty-nine and a half, her résumé read like a menu from the Cheesecake Factory: long, eclectic, and impossible to summarize. She had founded a legal tech start-up, earned a master's in fine arts, worked in nonprofit advocacy, dabbled in media consulting, and briefly considered a career in journalism. Each pivot made sense in the moment. Each one carried a flicker of promise. But none of them stuck.

She had always been a high achiever. Raised in a suburb of New Jersey, Chelsea was the daughter of an overbearing father who found his career path early and expected the same of her and her three older brothers. She was academically gifted, excelling in both economics and journalism electives during her college years at Northwestern.

Chelsea had been an account director at a creative media agency for the last year but hadn't fully settled in. Each new idea she explored came with a rush of excitement, followed by a wave of doubt. She began building a pitch deck for her own media agency start-up, then lost faith in the concept. She got into business school and then deferred twice. She filled journals with brainstorms, took countless networking calls, and enrolled in multiple online courses.

She became an expert in researching purpose but felt no closer to living it.

When she showed up to our calls, I never knew what version of Chelsea I was going to get. Sometimes she appeared bright-eyed, with her long brown hair in a slick back ponytail and a light dusting of makeup. Other times, she showed up ten minutes late looking like she'd just rolled out of bed. Her physical appearance mirrored her internal state, whether she was feeling motivated and inspired at work, or feeling lost and adrift.

When she wore the same Northwestern shirt for our third meeting in a row and looked dejected, I asked her how she was feeling. "It feels like my accelerator is broken," she said. "I've revved my engine so many times that it's given out."

As she neared her fortieth birthday, Chelsea began to feel the weight of what she hadn't committed to. "My whole life, I've been searching for my thing," she said. "My dad found his purpose young and built a fifty-year career. My three older brothers locked into their paths early. I'm the one still wandering. I feel like the black sheep of the family."

When I asked her what she pictured when she imagined her ideal career, she looked away. "I don't know," she said quietly. "That question makes me feel like a failure."

This is common among Seekers. Many were raised in environments with strong external influences, such as parents, siblings, or mentors, who taught them to prioritize logic and achievement over intuition. Over time, they stopped trusting their inner voice. Chelsea had spent decades looking for answers in programs, experts, and structured paths, always believing someone else had the answer she couldn't find on her own.

So I tried something different. I asked Chelsea, "What if you did know? What if you let the part of you that already knows speak? What would she say?"

She closed her eyes. After a long pause, she said, "Part of me wants a quiet life rescuing animals on a farm, but I would miss my family too much if I moved away. Another part of me wants to settle down, get married, have kids, and do nonprofit work. Another part of me wants to build a multimillion-dollar company with a passionate cofounder. And some days, I want to make documentaries. I'm all over the place."

To Chelsea, this was proof that she was broken. To me, it was proof that she was alive. Her ideas weren't the problem. Her fear of choosing was. She was holding herself to an impossible standard. She believed there was one right path, one perfect decision that would unlock her purpose and fulfillment. She believed that until she found it, she couldn't be happy.

Seekers can also fall into a pit of compare and despair, thinking everyone else has it figured out or has "their thing." This can further exacerbate a feeling of isolation and a determination to find the fulfillment that everyone else has access to. Their thinking that other people have it figured out or "know best" makes Seekers especially vulnerable to seductive promises—self-discovery retreats, the advanced degree, the business idea—that claim to cure it all. Even in my work with my Seeker clients, I have to be careful not to position myself as a guru or my coaching as a cure-all.

Chelsea also carried a heavy spiritual weight. She had long believed that she was born with a specific purpose and that not discovering or activating that purpose meant she was letting herself and God down. "Have you ever read the children's book *Are You My Mother?*" she asked one day. "I feel like that little bird, wandering around, asking every job, every class, every business idea, 'Are you my purpose? Are you my purpose?'" Conflating a career with purpose can be inspiring for some, but for Seekers like Chelsea it feels more of a burden than an inspiration.

Chelsea's story is at the heart of the Seeker wound. The pain is not a lack of ambition. It is an abundance of it, tangled in fear, shame, and inherited expectations. She didn't know it yet, but it was this Seeker mentality that would become her greatest strength, channeling her search for a singular purpose into seeking her True Self.

She gave herself permission to release the myth of the perfect path. She asked herself new questions. *What lights me up, even a little? What part of this idea feels real, not performative? What would I pursue if success were guaranteed?*

Once she began to trust herself and loosen the grip of comparison, she stopped searching for her path and began walking it. But before she could do that, her first step was to understand what deeper wound was holding her back.

THE SEEKER CHEAT SHEET

Motivation:

Driven by the belief that fulfillment lies in the next job.

They love it when you call them:

- A visionary
- Persuasive
- Capable of anything

The gifts:

- Imaginative: They have an abundance of new ideas.
- Leadership: They can galvanize support for their inspiring vision.
- Connection: Their variety of experiences often allows them to connect with many different types of people.

The shadow:

- Compare and despair
- Restless, unable to stay present and enjoy where they are
- Shiny object syndrome (chasing the next best thing)
- Outsource their intuition and inner guidance to others

THE PLEASER

As a Pleaser, you are motivated by maintaining positive workplace relationships, often at your own expense. You're gifted, deeply empathetic, and instinctively attuned to what others need. For Pleasers, the ultimate prize is being liked, and any threat to that approval can send you spiraling: *What did I say wrong? What does their delay in response mean?*

This was true for Talia, who explained, "I need constant reassurance that my team likes me. Even though I'm the boss, I find myself scared to give them direct feedback, scared they'll quit and say bad things about me and the company."

Talia had built a life around being indispensable. She was sharp, thoughtful, and deeply admired. On paper, she looked like a model of professional success. She had risen quickly, becoming the director of advertising at just thirty-two years old, admired for her calm presence, her ability to deliver under pressure, and her reputation for always being available. She was the person everyone could count on to come through, smooth things over, and pick up the slack. Her smile was wide and bright; she also never wore the same shade of lipstick or the same earrings twice, which delighted me to no end.

But under the polish was a constant hum of anxiety. In our first session, she admitted, "If someone doesn't like me, I might die or disappear." She wasn't being dramatic. That fear lived deep in her nervous system, and it had been driving her for years.

Talia grew up in Houston, the daughter of parents who immigrated from Algeria. As a Black girl growing up in Texas, she experienced racism and always felt different. "School felt like a science experiment. I became a master observer, constantly scanning for what people wanted from me. I would chameleon and code switch to give other people what they wanted from me," Talia explained.

Pleasers often come from challenging or chaotic homes, shaped by parents who were unpredictable or emotionally volatile. For Talia, home was once filled with life and love. That changed when her mother died young, and Talia was forced to grow up quickly, taking care of her three younger siblings while her father worked and struggled with his own grief. Determined not to let her grief define her, she made a silent pact with herself that as soon as she left the house, she would start living for *her*.

Throughout her career, her peers and managers praised her as "reliable," "committed," and "the glue of the team." But when we reviewed the positive feedback from a 360 performance review, her eyes welled with tears—not from pride, but from exhaustion.

"All I hear in those words," she told me, "are the late nights, the tasks that weren't mine, the way I bend myself into someone who never lets people down. I've trained everyone to expect I'll handle it. I don't ever want to disappoint people or have them question why I am in this role and ten years younger than most peers."

Two commonly combined Unfulfilled Achiever archetypes are the Pleaser and the Grinder. It's the desire to please that urges these Grinders to work. Often driven by the need to be liked for their usefulness, these individuals tend to express love through acts of service. In order to avoid feelings of inadequacy and maintain favor, they grind, hustle, and overwork. Talia took on her team's work like a camel, throwing endless to-dos on her back, making her load heavier and heavier, all out of fear of disappointing her boss, who'd promoted her and believed in her.

Giving direct feedback made her skin crawl; so instead, she picked up the slack herself. "I'll just do it" was her motto. Motivated by connection, Pleasers can often confuse managing with caretaking, which can prevent them from providing feedback to their reports and lead to taking on others' work, or being overly empathetic, allowing others to take advantage of them.

Talia was not only a Pleaser but one of the kindest and most accomplished people I had ever met. You don't have to be conventionally nice to be a Pleaser; many are quietly seething with resentment because no one takes care of *them*.

Talia's sorrow, laced with resentment, made her feel like Dr. Jekyll and Mr. Hyde. On the surface, she was agreeable and always said she was "happy to help," but inside she felt anything but happy. She craved approval and praise from her colleagues but resented what it took to earn it—always saying yes, anticipating needs, and doing everything for everyone. Frustration is a frequent companion for Pleasers who feel that their time, energy, and entire self exist solely for other people's gain. Their anger signals that a boundary has been crossed, but they don't know which one. Pleasers may set boundaries at first, but they often struggle to maintain a clear line between themselves and others.

Returning to the feedback, Talia said tearfully, "If I'm known as an intuitive leader who can anticipate other people's needs and deliver with a smile, that's great for *them*. But who is doing that for *me*? No one. I feel alone and helpless, like I need help but have no one to turn to."

That's the irony of the Pleaser: In their attempts to maintain connection, they lose themselves and feel more alone than ever. Trading authenticity for attachment is a losing bargain; both sides end up with less.

In childhood, Pleasers learned early that to stay connected and in the good graces of their caregivers, they needed to repress their needs and authenticity. In attachment theory, a psychological understanding of how humans make connections as determined by early childhood experiences, Pleasers often have anxious attachment styles, causing them to feel fearful and codependent. For Talia and many Pleasers, over-functioning is a coping mechanism. They do more than their share to avoid conflict or disconnection because if a relationship ruptures, it might expose their deepest fear: that they're not good enough, not capable, or don't belong.

A Pleaser's response to the pain of their success wound is to create a semblance of safety through being liked. As a result, Pleasers feel intense discomfort when others are upset with them or when they believe they are the cause of someone's unhappiness. So it's no surprise that setting a boundary with a boss, client, or family member can send Pleasers into an anxiety spiral, feeling deeply insecure.

I relate to this deeply. Today, as a career coach, my success wound most commonly shows up in Pleaser tendencies. I can confuse my clients' approval for my business success, thinking that the more I win them over, the more likely they are to recommend my services to their friends or think highly of me as a person. A few years ago, I had a client who intimidated me. She spoke harshly, calling her boss an idiot because he hadn't agreed with her and labeling her colleagues "pathetic" for self-promoting. I held back in sharing what I saw as her limiting patterns—judgment, black-and-white thinking, lack of collaboration—because I feared her judgment turning on me. I was scared that if she didn't like what I said, she wouldn't like *me*.

When I brought this up to a mentor, she reframed the situation for me. She said, "Your job is to hold up a mirror. They might not like what they see, and that's where your compassion can come in. You can't do your job and pursue their approval at the same time. It clouds the mirror." The more that Pleasers like me and Talia can separate our value from our likability and our worth from other people's projections, the more we actually enjoy our work and our colleagues.

For Talia, her turning point came when she began to question the belief at the root of it all: that being liked was necessary for being safe. Reliable, intuitive, empathetic, and driven by connection, Pleasers have so much to give. Talia's story reveals the heart of the Pleaser archetype. Her patterns were not signs of weakness. They were survival strategies—deeply intelligent responses to the systems and messages that shaped her. But as she reclaimed her agency, she stopped bending to be chosen and started standing in the truth of her own worth. She didn't need to be everything to everyone. She needed to be someone to herself.

PLEASER CHEAT SHEET

Motivation:

Belief that being liked and approved of will bring the safety, belonging, and control they long for.

They love it when you call them:

- A team player
- An empathetic leader
- Easy to be around

The gifts:

- Empathetic: They genuinely care about how other people feel.
- Reliable: They will follow through on what they say.
- Intuitive: They are attuned to people's energies and needs.

The shadow:

- Their sense of worth often rises and falls with the most recent feedback from a manager or superior.
- They regularly put others' needs ahead of their own, leading to resentment and burnout.
- Anxiety around workplace relationships can lead to sleepless nights and days spent spiraling into self-doubt.
- They constantly feel unappreciated.

THE WORK HARD, PLAY HARD

The Work Hard, Play Hard wants to live life to the fullest, collecting as many peak experiences as possible. Living for novelty and thrill, they seek excellence in all things: their work performance, their play, and their rest. They want to be anything but ordinary, chasing the extraordinary with a "you only live once" urgency.

The constant pressure to excel creates internal stress that they often release through escapism, like partying, lots of alcohol, overeating, excessive shopping, gambling. It could also mean cramming life to the brim with too many commitments, leaving a wake of depletion. Work Hard, Play Hards keep themselves constantly booked and busy to avoid the quiet voice inside that whispers, *Something's not right here.*

That voice was getting louder for Joy, and she couldn't silence it.

Joy was introduced to me by a former client who, in her connecting email, not so subtly said, "Joy could *really* use your help."

Joy was the founder and CEO of an insurance brokerage outside San Antonio, Texas, and wanted me to know it. She told me, "I've built this business from scratch, and now we're the top brokerage in the city, on our way to expanding across the state this year." Her days were packed with meetings, strategy sessions, and high-stakes decisions. She ran her company with the precision of a Navy SEAL, kept her team moving at a rapid pace, and managed her personal life with the same level of efficiency. She described herself as someone who could outwork anyone, and she often did.

I oohed and aahed at all the right places, but I could sense an underlying franticness to Joy's energy. She added that she was PTA president, which took up a ton of time but was really worth it, and she'd just finished a home renovation on a farm, no less, with two horses, three pigs, and a pair of goats on the way.

After her rehearsed introduction was over, I paused and took a deep breath. I felt her manic drive thrum in my own chest. I paused and let the silence settle. Joy forced a smile and shifted in her seat, clearly uncomfortable with the stillness that followed the reading of her accomplishments. The words poured out of my mouth before I knew what they were. "What are you running from, Joy?"

Her eyes flickered as she seemed to weigh the pros and cons of being honest or deflecting the question. She looked down at her hands, fiddling with the five rings stacked on her left ring finger. "I don't know," she finally whispered. "But whatever it is, I've been running from it my whole life."

How so? I wondered. As we talked, Joy began to open up. "Staying busy is one way I run. Another is by pouring myself a glass of wine and going out to clean the horse stalls for hours to avoid my husband. I find myself going to the fridge when I'm stressed, even when I'm not hungry. I treat myself to fabulous spa weekends with my sister-in-law, hoping to unwind, but I never actually do. I'm living this surface-level life that looks good but feels a bit... empty."

On paper, or at least in her annual Christmas card, Joy appeared successful, fulfilled, and put together. She always showed up to our sessions with her beautiful red hair cut into a coiffed bob. Pictures of her equally beautiful family on their farm lined her desk. The disconnect between how life looks and how it feels creates a gnawing, existential anxiety that many Work Hard, Play Hards do their best to avoid.

I nodded, feeling the deep ache of recognition. When my inner Work Hard, Play Hard was running the show, I'd never felt emptier. That hollowness was so uncomfortable because I was ashamed that it was there in the first place. How could I possibly feel like something's missing if I have so much? I had an education, a job, a family that loves me. Why wasn't this enough? I recognized this shame in Joy as well. This anxiety used to eat me from the inside. I was compelled to relieve both the pressure I felt to succeed and the shame that, even with success, I still felt deficient. Partying became this release for me.

Work Hard, Play Hards, like Joy and me, conflate play with escapism. Your distractions can show up as gaming, TV, social media, dating, porn, sex, drinking, overeating, undereating, fantasy, travel, shopping, sports betting, and so much more. It's not the form your escapism takes; it's whether you're using it as a means to manage or ignore a deeper issue within that actually needs your attention.

"I overindulge and beat myself up for it. It's like this part of my brain throws a temper tantrum after a hard day of taking care of people and working. It thinks it's entitled to some fun, too. Fun is one of my core values; I love bringing humor and levity into situations. Without fun, what's the point?" she beamed.

I could easily see how Joy's charisma and enthusiasm made her an inspiring leader and a magnetic colleague, keenly able to win others over. In our sessions, Joy began to trace the connection between her pain and the constant pressure she placed on herself. She had long assumed that reward was something to be earned only after exhaustive effort. Her so-called playtime, including weekend wine, online shopping, and elaborate trips, was how she self-soothed. But it was also her only access to pleasure. She realized she was not enjoying her life. She was recovering from it.

Many of my clients are also working mothers who rely on the Work Hard, Play Hard strategy. They all describe their substance of choice as their only consistent source of pleasure. They seek pleasure as a means to balance out the pain of their success wound. Unconsciously, these working moms live in a constant seesaw between exhaustion and pain on one side and pleasure and reward on the other.

The "Work Hard" part of this type has Grinder tendencies, like Joy does. But the Grinder and the Work Hard, Play Hard differ in both their primary motivation and in their method of anesthetizing discomfort. Work Hard, Play Hards are motivated by intensity, variety, and high achievement. They desire the best in all areas—how they work, unwind, and recover. Grinders, by contrast, are driven by the need to prove their value through productivity. Both types experience the success wound's pain of feeling deeply deficient in some way. Grinders blot out the pain by working even harder, trying to prove their worth through productivity. Work Hard, Play Hards, on the other hand, escape through excitement, substances, and a constant drive to "treat yourself."

Maybe you had a phase of being a Work Hard, Play Hard in your twenties or early thirties and now identify more with another type (like Grinder or Pleaser). If so, take another look at the role of play in your life. How do you relax? Is it the same way you push down unwanted feelings or avoid discomfort? How have you found new ways to blow off steam as you've grown? Is pleasure your right or something to be earned?

Joy's story captures the essence of the Work Hard, Play Hard pattern. It is not simply about working long hours or enjoying nice things. It is about the more profound fear that without constant motion or achievement, we are not enough. But when that belief is healed, what remains is someone deeply capable, creative, and finally able to experience pleasure that does not need to be earned through exhaustion.

This became the beginning of a new relationship with the part of her that had always pushed for more. She stopped trying to overpower it and began to understand it. What was it afraid of? What was it trying to protect her from? She realized it had been shielding her from shame, from the fear that if she wasn't exceptional, she didn't matter. This was confronting for Joy, who struggled to reconcile these darker feelings with her sunny disposition.

When clients like Joy channel that positivity and a can-do attitude into an earnest desire for change in their life, they are unstoppable.

WORK HARD, PLAY HARD CHEAT SHEET

Motivation:

A belief that the harder they push at work, the more they deserve to escape through equally intense forms of play.

They love it when you call them:

- The life of the office (or the party)
- The hustler
- Extraordinary, enviable, successful

The gifts:

- The "yes" person: They are always eager to give a little extra—whether that means staying late to finish a project or sticking around for one more round at happy hour.
- Variety of experiences: By saying yes to numerous opportunities, they often accumulate rich experiences and build a wide, well-connected network.
- Sensitive and intuitive: Their natural sensitivity often drives the urge to numb through constant busyness and overstimulation.

The shadow:

- Difficulty finding sustainable work-life balance
- Superficial sense of fulfillment
- Prone to addictive behaviors; they numb out in unhealthy ways and call it "self-care"

YOU ALREADY HAVE WHAT IT TAKES TO BE FREE

You might feel at odds with your ambition or unsure of your strength—but there's something magnetic about you and about women like you. Regardless of your type, you are looking for fulfillment, belonging, greatness, and significance—even if you've been looking in the wrong places. What matters is the drive to seek. Your ambition is an inner fire that's irresistibly engaging and appealing. You see the world through a lens of innovation (*What could be better here?*), of possibility (*Could I do that? I could do that.*), and of connection (*How can I find common ground with this person?*). Each type contains a ticket to a new freedom and inner peace you've never known. The key is to find an inner leader who can direct these unfulfilled parts of you into a harmonious symphony. That inner leader is your True Self, the part of you that knows how to work from fulfillment, not disillusionment; satisfaction, not emptiness; sustainability, not burnout.

CHAPTER 3

THE WOUNDED SELF, PROTECTOR SELF, AND TRUE SELF

Your Problem Is Singular and So Is Your Solution

Sutton felt like she was losing an inner battle with herself. She signed into our virtual session about three months into working together, looking distraught. "Well, it finally happened. It seems the Universe or whatever has forced my hand," she said sarcastically. "My team has been dissolved, and they gave me two options: take a less senior role on a sister team or a severance package. And I have absolutely no idea what to do."

For Sutton, this news was both a blessing and a curse. She had been at the investment bank her whole career and most of her identity was wrapped up in it. Of course her family back home in Louisiana came first, but beyond that, her job meant everything to her, from her livelihood to how she conceived of her daily routine, walking the twenty-two minutes to work along the Charles River in Boston, and seeing the trees change with the seasons. More than a paycheck, her sense of place in the world was informed by being an employee at this company. And yet Sutton was completely burnt out from both the office politics and from the challenge of trying to balance her personal life with a job that seemed to ask more and more of her each year.

Over the last three months, we had talked at length about the push and pull between her desire to find a new job and reinvent herself professionally, and her pull toward the safety and certainty that her job offered. "It feels like there are three different Suttons all arguing inside me," she said.

In our coaching work, we identified her inner Hider that said, *I can't possibly start a new career path at this point. What if I can't find another job and can't pay my mortgage?* She also had an inner Pleaser that chimed in with *My mentors and managers have poured so much energy into me. Will they think I'm ungrateful or lazy if I take the severance?* These voices had long shaped Sutton's career, dictating how quickly she replied to client emails and how rarely she prioritized her social life. Her Hider and Pleaser called the shots in her career, making it impossible to locate what she truly wanted.

But beyond the anxious hand-wringing of these two voices was a third voice that was as clear as a tuning fork. The voice spoke to her through the tension and fatigue she felt in her body when she considered taking the job offer on a sister team. The voice came through an inspiring feeling that surged through her body when she spoke to a former colleague who left finance behind to be a freelance strategy consultant. The voice came in thoughts of possibility: *There's something exciting about the unknown.* Almost as soon as this voice spoke up, her Hider's voice of practicality would jump in: *But I would be irresponsible to take a severance package without another job lined up.*

I asked Sutton if she knew who or what this voice of calm confidence was. "It's . . . *me*," she responded clearly. "There's a knowing in that voice, like when I accepted the job in Boston without ever having been to Massachusetts. Or when I walked into the apartment I now own and my whole body immediately recognized it as home. It's the inner knowing that I trusted to end my last relationship. When I know something is right or when I am clear on the next right action it feels solid and tangible, not hollow and anxious. I know the right next step for me because it is the next right step for me." I nodded and smiled.

When Sutton follows this voice of clarity, her life unfolds naturally. When I asked her then to close her eyes and remember what it felt like to listen to this voice, she said that it was "like gliding through life instead of pushing or stumbling through. It feels like a giant exhale." This voice carried the answers, not only to the "Should I stay or should I go?" question, but to all the other career decisions, worries, and anxieties that plagued her daily.

Perhaps you've also experienced a chorus of voices within you, each with its own values and motivations, often pulling you in different directions. You might notice it during moments of internal conflict—like feeling the urge to chase an ambitious deadline while another part of you just wants to take it easy. For Sutton, one voice urged her to hold tight to the stable finance job, while another recognized how holding tight was holding her back. It was a third, quieter and wiser voice that she had to listen to in order to take the next step in her career. That same voice is the one you'll need to access to find the fulfillment and satisfaction you're seeking.

So, what are these parts of you? And how do they hold you back or help you move forward?

THE THREE SELVES

Our psyches are made up of distinct parts. Drawing from Gestalt psychology and Internal Family Systems therapy, I use a simple but powerful framework of the three selves: the Wounded Self, which carries unresolved pain; the Protector Self, which compensates by seeking control and safety; and the True Self, our calm, clear inner leader. These parts interact, often leaving us stuck in cycles of overwork and self-doubt.

Richard Schwartz began developing IFS in 1984 while working as a family therapist, where he counseled multiple family members in a single session. Over time, he observed that each individual seemed to have their own internal "family," made up of different "parts" or subpersonalities. These parts can have diverging motivations, perspectives, and beliefs about how you should react or run your life. These differing voices within can make you feel like you're arguing with yourself or thinking in loops. For Sutton, some of these parts were her inner Hider (that wanted her to stay in a predictable finance job), her Pleaser (that didn't want to disappoint her mentors or her family), and the voice of her inner clarity (that yearned to grow and explore a new career path).

The True Self is your innate source of confidence, clarity, and fulfillment. It's the voice of your intuition, your inner knowing, that is always guiding you toward your highest potential and the most optimal path for you. Sutton experienced her inner knowing at pivotal moments in her life, like when she moved to Boston sight unseen, or the first time she walked into her apartment. It's also the flow state that comes from devoting your focus and energy to something you love. The energized buzz that's generated and shared during an inspiring brainstorming session. When we work from our True Self, we can't help but be inspired, successful, and satisfied.

Yet throughout life, we all accumulate wounds, big and small. The Wounded Self is another part of us, one that carries these moments of rejection, abandonment, or trauma (like your parent leaving forever or experiencing or witnessing abuse). Painful experiences in our careers can cause wounds, too. For example, moments when we experienced embarrassment after a public failure, bullying from a toxic manager, maternal or racial bias, the trauma of severe burnout, and more. In IFS, these are called exiled parts of us that hide in the recesses of our unconscious mind. This wound is afraid to be hurt again. But it also longs to be seen, acknowledged, and brought out of the shadows.

Over time, we develop habits at work to protect us from failure, embarrassment, or conflict that might resurface the Wounded Self's pain. It could be taking on extra projects despite being at capacity because you want to seem like a team player, staying in a stagnant job for a decade because it feels safe and familiar, or nodding in agreement even when everything inside you says it's wrong. These are examples of your Protector Self at work. The Unfulfilled Achiever within you is part of your Protector Self trying to keep you safe.

At work and throughout our careers, the Protector Self shields us from vulnerability by adopting Unfulfilled Achiever strategies. Over time, we confuse these protective behaviors with who we are. We claim, "I'm a perfectionist." "I'm a workaholic." "I'm a people pleaser." "I'm analytical and unemotional." The more we identify with this armor, the further we separate from our True Self, causing an unconscious longing to reconnect with who we really are, but we don't know how.

In Sutton's case, the Hider and Pleaser archetypes (which are part of her Protector Self) drove her decisions and kept her on a singular career path within finance. Now, forced to make a decision at this juncture in her career—to stay or go—she was confronted with who to listen to: the familiar voice of her Hider that urged her to do the responsible thing, or the expansive feeling of her True Self that had a budding curiosity about what else could be possible.

These three selves form the internal system behind your thoughts, choices, and habits. The success wound is formed by the dynamic between the Wounded Self, which carries pain and unmet needs, and the Protector Self, which compensates by seeking control, achievement, and external validation. The Wounded Self whispers, *I'm not enough*, and the Protector Self responds, *I know how to fix this.* It relies on conformity, relentless hard work, control, achievement, and constant productivity to shield against the pain of feeling unworthy as she truly is. These two parts of you reinforce the belief that you're not enough unless you are overworking, avoiding failure, booked and busy, or constantly succeeding.

This is a trap many women fall into: abandoning their True Self in pursuit of belonging. In *The Heroine's Journey: Women's Quest for Wholeness*, author, professor, and psychotherapist Maureen Murdock describes this as an inward, psychospiritual quest for wholeness. While Joseph Campbell's hero's journey begins with a call to adventure, Murdock's heroine's journey starts when a woman forsakes her True Self—including her femininity—in order to conform to a patriarchal model of success. As Murdock puts it, women often "choose to follow a model of success that denies who they are."[1]

As long as your Protector Self is calling the shots, true career fulfillment will keep slipping through your fingers. The Protector Self is driven by fear, control, and external validation—not by your true desires or values. It keeps you in a cycle of overworking and striving, hoping that success will finally bring a sense of relief from the constant questioning if you're doing enough.

Your True Self can be obscured by your Unfulfilled Achiever parts but never broken or damaged. It is always there. Beyond the self-doubt and fear of failure or the obsessive need to check your email. Just past the anxiety that crashes in when you think about leaving your toxic job, there is an inner resource that knows how to find career freedom.

Your True Self Can Heal Your Success Wound

Lasting fulfillment can only come from reconnecting with your True Self. Without this connection, no amount of achievement will ever feel like enough. The aim of this book is to help you find your True Self as the rightful leader of your inner world. The magic of this work lies in the profound transformation that happens when you reconnect with this innate leader—the part of you that holds wisdom, strength, and compassion. Once this connection is made, something remarkable begins: The success wound you've carried for years can start to loosen its grip. The fear and pain that once motivated you starts to dissolve, making space for clarity, peace, and even joy.

This was Sutton's experience. She came to this work feeling burdened by old stories of responsibility and duty, locking her in a pattern of self-doubt that blocked her ability to see the next step in her career. But through the process of reconnecting with her inner healer, she discovered something she hadn't known was possible—a way to hold her past without being held captive by it. Her success wound, once raw and consuming, began to release its pain—not because it was forgotten, but because it was finally acknowledged, understood, and healed from within. Sutton's turning point didn't come all at once, but when it came, it was well worth the effort (which we will unpack in Chapters 6 and 7). Her inner Hider naturally stepped aside once it trusted that the True Self can take care.

The essence of healing is not in erasing our past experiences but changing the way we carry them. When the True Self leads, healing becomes more than a possibility—it becomes inevitable. Understanding your brain's wiring can help you harness that inevitability.

The Neuroscience of the Three Selves: Responsive and Reactive Mode

Another reason our success wounds have been leading the way? We're wired for it. There's a neurological explanation for why we default to negative beliefs and why the persona of our Unfulfilled Achiever becomes a habitual way of working.

The brain is built to automatically react when it senses a potential threat, triggering a stress response in the body. Our brains tend to live in reactive mode—state of emergency!—as we scan for possible reasons why we might be criticized or critiqued, miss the mark, or drop a ball. For my clients working in toxic environments marred by gossip, back-channeling, or cutthroat competition, their nervous systems are often in overdrive, constantly perceiving threats.

These moments of acute stress are when our Unfulfilled Achievers leap into action to protect us from the threat of disconnection or lack of safety, or to search for satisfaction. If you think back to the last time your Grinder or Hider or Pleaser showed up in its most severe mode, I'm guessing it was a period of stress when you'd received a strongly worded email or felt overwhelmed by a to-do list that just wouldn't end.

While Sutton's primary strategy is to hide whenever she feels pressure at work—whether from her demanding boss or an impossible deadline—her Pleaser and Grinder would leap into action, pushing her to overdeliver, overextend, and overanalyze every task. To her, this felt like a natural response to stress, but in reality it was her Unfulfilled Achievers working overtime to ensure she felt safe, accepted, and in control.

Yet, despite all her efforts, satisfaction remained elusive. Years earlier, she'd hoped that the promotion from associate to vice president would bring a more substantial change in her daily responsibilities, like managing people or setting strategy, which would reengage her interest. The pride from her promotion wore off as quickly as a sugar hit. She felt a mix of stress from increased responsibility and also boredom. "It turns out, a promotion can't make me like finance. Nor can it make me more confident," she joked. But she kept on. The more her Pleaser and Grinder took charge, the more disconnected she felt from herself.

It wasn't until Sutton began to recognize these patterns and understand their origins that she could start loosening their grip. By reconnecting with her True Self—the part of her that didn't need constant validation to feel worthy—she began to rewrite her story. In senior executive meetings, she summoned the courage to speak up twice more than she typically would have. Instead of defaulting to her Unfulfilled Achiever in moments of overwhelm, Sutton learned to pause, breathe, and respond with intention. She started to feel more confident at work, which spilled over into other areas of her life. Gradually, her brain formed new pathways, helping her meet stress with calm, self-compassion, and clarity. From this state of regulation, she could finally hear the answer that was right for her. She opted to take the severance.

This is the gift of pursuing aligned ambition. It allows you to transform those five-alarm-fire moments of stress, when our Unfulfilled Achievers try to take over, into opportunities to pause, listen to what our intuition is telling us, and bravely take steps in that direction. The goal is not to eradicate stress entirely but to learn how to meet it differently, with greater awareness and trust in your capabilities.

NEGATIVITY BIAS

Our brains have a built-in negativity bias where we learn more from painful experiences and negative interactions than from pleasurable or positive ones. This bias causes us to focus on real or imagined slights from a colleague or a piece of critical feedback while ignoring the more frequent positive interactions or praise from a week ago. For instance, if your boss makes a flippant remark about how your colleague is performing incredibly well, you might become hyper-aware and draw a comparison between yourself and your colleague, searching for signs that indicate your boss is dissatisfied with you or that you're falling behind. According to research from the Gottman Institute, we need five positive experiences to outweigh the impact of just one negative one.[2] Even if your boss is generally supportive, your brain may fixate on that one negative remark, viewing it as a serious threat to your sense of security and connection. Negativity bias is also contagious within teams. If you've worked on a team that was under pressure to deliver, or at a company in a state of hyper-growth, you likely sensed the defensiveness, reactivity, and poor decision-making that swept through your colleagues like a bad cold. It's not our fault that we are hardwired for negativity. But you *do* have a choice in how you respond.

When you slow down and reconnect with your inner authority, the change doesn't just happen in your thoughts but in your body. Your brain shifts out of its habitual stress response and into a calmer, more receptive state, where insight, creativity, and strategic thinking begin to surface. This is the parasympathetic nervous system at work—not just "rest and digest," but recalibrate and repair. Your heart rate slows. Your breath deepens. In that safety, your mind can make space for emotion, and your system can begin to heal. (You can experience this through the exercise on page 101.) From this state of regulation, it's much easier to respond to everyday work issues with confidence, like giving difficult feedback, presenting to senior stakeholders, crafting an ambitious annual strategy, or making a big career decision.

Tuning into your True Self isn't just about calm—it's about working intentionally. At work you navigate tough situations with a foundation of security. You are no longer working on autopilot or from emotional reactions. You can access new ideas and insightful perspectives, and act as a leader even when others are stressed and defensive.

When I explain this to my clients, sometimes they object, saying, "But I need to be a bit anxious at work—it keeps me on my toes," or "I don't want to let go of my grinding tendencies completely." They're not wrong! Healing your success wound gives you the *choice* in how you work. You can keep the strength of your Grinder and minimize the suffering. You can grind it out when needed and then toggle back into the responsive mode of your True Self; you can keep some necessary performance anxiety around before a big presentation without letting it run your life.

Every moment you're faced with this very choice: to move through your workday from your Wounded and Protector Selves or to respond from your True Self. If you don't choose that deeper alignment, your nervous system will do it for you—pulling you into old stress patterns, catastrophizing, or seeing everyone or everything as a threat. You'll brace against life rather than meet it. However, this isn't a onetime decision. It's a daily, moment-by-moment practice, a relearning of how to think, feel, and work from a place of wholeness rather than fear.

YOUR TRUE SELF NATURALLY COMES FORWARD WHEN YOUR CORE NEEDS ARE MET

Fortunately, our brains also have the wiring to access our True Self. According to Rick Hanson in *Hardwiring Happiness*, the brain has three main needs: security, satisfaction, and connection. When there is a sense that these needs are met—when we're safe, content, and connected—our brain shifts into a responsive mode, calming the body and activating the parasympathetic nervous system. In this state, we gain perspective, regulate emotions more effectively, and approach challenges with greater creativity and trust in ourselves and in others.[3]

We do this by training our brain to recognize that these needs are met. For example, we can feel connected to ourselves and our colleagues, even if there are moments of disconnection. We can reframe challenges or threatening moments as neutral (or even as opportunities). We are satisfied with what we have, and how our work is going because we've set our own standards for what is good and enough. By being present in the moment, we can feel safe even if the future is uncertain.

Your Turn: An Easy Way to Tap into Your True Self Energy

Read through the instructions first, and then try it yourself. I suggest first practicing this visualization in a neutral environment (like where you're reading this book right now). Then practice this at work in moments of stress, overwhelm, or frustration to return to the regulation and responsive mode of your True Self. I have been known to practice this in a work bathroom or on a brief walk outside (with eyes open).

1. Start by looking around your environment, noticing the physical aspects of your surroundings. Notice that you're in a safe environment where your need for **safety** is met. You might repeat to yourself a few times, "I am safe. All is well," until you believe it.
2. Then close your eyes. Take a few deep breaths, bringing your focus inward. Count five things in your life that fill you with a sense of **satisfaction**. Consider your health, your last piece of good feedback, the last time you did something courageous or beat the odds.
3. Finally, with your eyes still closed, think of the three most important relationships in your life—a friend, a pet, your partner, kids, parents, or a mentor. Think about the beautiful quality of your **connection**: how you two met, how you feel around them, and your gratitude for their presence in your life.
4. Notice how this feels in your body. Do your shoulders drop? Does your jaw soften? Do you feel an opening in your chest or a lightness in your limbs?
5. Now turn inward. What emotions are present in your mind or heart?
6. Stay with the feeling. Let it wash over you and notice how your body, mind, and spirit respond.

7. This state where your needs are met—that deep calm, clarity, and connection—is your True Self.
8. Now imagine working *from* this state. Imagine delivering the tough feedback to your report from a state of calm and connection or responding to the passive-aggressive email knowing that you're safe. That's how you work *from* strength.

You can download an audio version of this visualization at www.brooketaylorcoaching.com/book

INSTINCT IS MORE IMPORTANT THAN INTELLECT, ACCORDING TO BUSINESS LEADERS

Whether it's Oprah Winfrey or Steve Jobs, thought leaders, creatives, and business minds across generations and industries have called their True Self by different names. But they all agree on its essential role in guiding us toward a more meaningful life.

Oprah attributes her extraordinary success and the lasting impact of her television show and media career to being "grounded in my own self," where her being fueled her doing.[4] Spiritual teacher and author Marianne Williamson describes this inner voice as a "natural intelligence"—a force within us, the same intelligence that transforms an acorn into an oak tree, guiding us toward our purpose.[5] Scholar Joseph Campbell famously referred to it as *bliss*, urging us to follow it. In the book *The Power of Myth*, he says, "If you do follow your bliss, you put yourself on a kind of track that has been there all the while, waiting for you, and the life that you ought to be living is the one you are living."[6]

Similarly, many innovators in the business world have credited their success to this inner guidance. Steve Jobs called it intuition, claiming it was more important than intellect in shaping his career and business triumphs. In his 2005 commencement address at Stanford University, Jobs said, "Have the courage to follow your heart and intuition. They somehow already know what you truly want to become. Everything else is secondary."[7] His successor at Apple, Tim Cook, faced a pivotal decision when considering whether to leave a secure position at Compaq to join Apple. His pro-con lists consistently pointed toward staying at Compaq. Yet, despite his analytical nature, he couldn't ignore the persistent voice of his intuition urging him to join Apple. Reflecting on this decision, Cook said in an interview at Duke University, "Even though I'm an engineer and an analytical person at heart, the most important decisions I've made had nothing to do with that. They always had to do with intuition."[8] Trusting that voice transformed his career and life.

Philosophers, too, have long pointed to this inner knowing. Plato believed that all knowledge originates from intuition and can be felt in our core as truth.

Whether you call it your intuition, your higher self, your inner knowing, your authentic self, or consciousness, the True Self is that part of you that knows who you are and where you are meant to go. I've seen it over and over: When clients listen to their True Self, their lives open. Work feels lighter. Big career decisions are made with greater trust. And purpose no longer feels like something they have to chase. It is from this state of being that we can work more collaboratively with others, problem solve creatively, and find intrinsic motivation that leads to better performance.

YOUR SOLUTION IS SINGULAR

This leads me to a confession: I say I'm a career coach who helps ambitious women like you find career fulfillment. That's only partially true. My real job is helping you reconnect with the fulfillment, joy, and satisfaction that's already alive within you. From there, the career puzzle of *What job I should take? How do I get promoted?* or *How should I best lead my team?*—it all tends to fall into place.

THE FASTEST WAY BACK TO YOUR SELF

Your True Self isn't just an abstract concept—you can shift your thoughts and behaviors to access it right in the here and now. You can fast-track yourself back into your True Self by identifying your values and core states of being, then ask yourself questions like *Am I behaving in alignment with my core values through this decision? Am I defaulting into my success wound? How can I come back into my core state of being right now?* By the end of this process, you'll not only gain clarity on what these terms mean to you but also develop the ability to apply them in high-stakes moments throughout your workday, empowering you to act from a place of authenticity, clarity, and calm.

YOUR CORE VALUES

We all hold certain values sacred. Principles that shape our choices, guide our relationships, and influence how we care for our health, finances, and overall well-being.

Our values spring either from our wounding or our wholeness. It is critical that the values come from our True Self, not our success wound. Each value should plug you into a state of possibility, empowerment, and potential. When you embody your values, you embody your higher state of being where the 8 C's of Self that we discussed in Chapter 1 (curiosity, compassion, calmness, clarity, confidence, courage, creativity, and connectedness) are present.

Take a few minutes to do the following exercise. But as you contemplate the list, try to avoid selecting values like security, control, and achievement (even though I'm sure you value achievement!), at least initially, because nine times out of ten they are coming from your success wound's need to control external things in order to feel safe. Remember, when we're grasping for control, we are in our Unfulfilled Achiever parts, and that leads to places like feeling stuck and burnt out.

Your Turn: Determine Your Top Values

Choose up to five core values from the list (or write your own). You may find that some of these naturally combine and that one word can suitably describe multiple others. For instance, if you value community, relationships, and service, you might say that Connection is one of your top values. You can reference the list on the next page for inspiration if you'd like. It is not an exhaustive list, so feel free to choose the word that resonates most with you.

TIP: If you imagine that value disappearing from your life and it *doesn't* give you a visceral reaction, it's not a core value. If you imagine it disappearing and you can't imagine your life without it, it is a core value.

Common Core Values

Abundance
Accountability
Adventure
Altruism
Authenticity
Autonomy
Balance
Boldness
Bravery
Challenge
Citizenship
Collaboration
Community
Compassion
Connection
Contribution
Courage
Creativity
Curiosity
Determination
Fairness
Faith
Freedom
Friendship
Fun
Growth
Happiness
Harmony
Health
Honesty
Humor
Influence
Integrity
Joy
Justice
Kindness
Knowledge
Leadership
Learning
Love
Loyalty
Meaning
Open-Mindedness
Openness
Optimism
Patriotism
Peace
Pleasure
Presence
Purpose
Religion
Resilience
Respect
Responsibility
Self-Respect
Service
Spirituality
True to Self
Trust
Well-Being
Wisdom

____

____

____

____

My Core Value . . .	*My Definition of This Value . . .*
______________________	______________________
______________________	______________________
______________________	______________________
______________________	______________________
______________________	______________________

You can download a digital version of this exercise at www.brooketaylorcoaching.com/book

I suggest writing these core values down someplace where you can see them daily. I want them to be ingrained in your mind the same way your mailing address and phone number are. These values are your new criteria for decision-making, for choosing how you respond or even what projects to take on at work. Ask yourself, *Am I acting from my core values here?* or *Is how I am showing up in this meeting/email/discussion in alignment with my values?* or even when you're feeling anxious or threatened: *How would my value of ________ respond to this email?*

On the other hand, when you look at your core values, you might see that they aren't present in your day-to-day at work. This might offer some explanation as to why you're not feeling lit up at work right now. That's okay. Allow that awareness to inspire you to seek out where your values *can* be met: on a new team, working with a new client or on a new project, or even in a new corporate culture.

YOUR CORE STATES OF BEING

Now that you've defined your core values, it's time to move them out of your head and into your body. I found that the first time I did a values exercise, I had a hard time translating my values from the page into my life. They felt conceptual and I wanted them to be practical. I also noticed when I was living my core value of *integrity* that I felt courageous, confident, and calm, even when this value required a difficult conversation. When I was living my core value of *freedom*, I felt light, unencumbered, and expansive in my body. These states of being sparked real, emotional, and physical shifts—the felt sense of being in alignment with my True Self.

We all pursue goals, not only for their attainment but for the *feeling* that we hope the goal will give us. Sutton pursued the promotion to vice president not only for the increased salary and new responsibilities but also to *feel* confident and proud. But these feelings wore off like a sugar hit. We can cultivate and create that feeling we want *now*, in our daily working life, not at the last step of the project or after the promotion.

I call this setting your core states of being. Decide how you want to *feel* at work and intentionally cultivating this feeling in your body can bring you back into alignment with your highest self.

I introduced core states of being to my client Chelsea, who most often defaulted into a Seeker type. When Chelsea was living in alignment with her values, she felt *satisfied*. "This is how I want work to feel most of the time," she told me. I urged her to start asking herself the question: *What can I do today that will make me feel satisfied?* instead of *What job would make me satisfied?* This switch took the pressure off the compulsive need to find the next role or the next project. Instead, she cultivated the feeling of satisfaction within her body through mindfulness. It plugged her back into her True Self and helped her reclaim her agency.

Your Turn:
Define Your Core States of Being

1. Look at your first core value. What does it feel like when you're fully living in alignment with it? Can you recall the last time you truly embodied this value in your life or work?
2. Close your eyes and bring that value into your heart. Reflect on its essence. What does this value truly mean to you beyond the word itself?
3. Allow your body to respond. Notice any sensations that arise, and observe the emotions that come with them.
4. Jot down the feelings that arise for each value. Some common feelings are: *ablaze, connected, curious, energized, grounded, free, flow, grateful, inspired.* Take your time moving through the list, one by one.
5. Review your list of feelings and states of being. Which ones light you up? Circle the ones that make you feel the most alive, connected, or fulfilled.

My Core States of Being Are…

We always have a choice in what part of us is driving our career. Authentic fulfillment isn't about what you do, it's about how you show up to the work you choose. That said, it can be difficult to tap into your True Self since we are hardwired to automatically default into our Protector Self and our success wound.

As you move into Part 2, you'll uncover practical tools to help you heal your success wound and let your True Self lead your career. You'll shift how you relate to your emotions, quiet overthinking and negativity bias, and adopt new ways of working that build you up rather than break you down. But before we get there, we need to explore what ambition looks like when it's driven by your True Self, not your success wound. This is what I call aligned ambition.

CHAPTER 4

ALIGNED AMBITION

A New Approach to Work and Fulfillment

You open your computer and that familiar sense of heaviness and dread washes over you. You see the pile of unanswered emails and a calendar full of meetings. The day has just started but you're already exhausted because you didn't sleep well after a night of worrying about an upcoming deadline and how it will all get done on time. So you race from meeting to meeting, anxiously trying to cross everything off your to-do list without making a mistake or saying the wrong thing.

For many of us, work feels like a chore. A daily uphill battle.

But when you embrace fulfillment as a state of being, work really can look like this:

You log into your computer, open your calendar, and genuinely look forward to your next meeting. In that meeting, you put forward your creative or controversial ideas because you know your perspective will make the work stronger. You reply directly to the irrational client with facts and confidence. Even in moments of stress, you can maintain a higher perspective without getting bogged down in details or frustration.

Outside opinions and projections become background noise. You're on your own path, running your own race, and that clarity fills you with confidence. That bigger picture of who you are becoming guides the smaller day-to-day decisions of your career.

The workplace becomes an arena of self-discovery, a space to uncover what you care about, and what you're capable of, all while building financial stability. When an exciting opportunity arises, you give it your all, fueled by passion, rather than agonizing worry. You understand that the process is just as meaningful as the outcome.

There's a new kind of balance in your life. Your center of gravity has shifted from your head to your heart. You're living your aligned ambition—and it shows.

If I had read that years ago, after a long day of office politics, hundreds of emails, and countless client demands, I would have rolled my eyes and dismissed it as unrealistic. I would have assumed it was written by someone who had never worked in a fast-paced organization, never had performance targets or KPIs (key performance indicators), or even knew what that acronym stood for. I would have questioned if this way of working could exist in a modern office culture where we don't necessarily get to pick our projects or our colleagues. My Work Hard, Play Hard achiever and this other way of being in aligned ambition would have felt like parallel universes, completely disconnected from each other.

Today I know this is possible, having lived it myself and seen my clients do the same by adopting new ways of being, thinking, and acting that connect their strengths, values, and desires with their bold ambition.

FULFILLMENT AND FLOW COME FROM ALIGNMENT

You've probably heard the word *alignment* in a variety of contexts. In business, it means syncing goals with mission. In car mechanics, it ensures smooth, steady movement. In Eastern medicine, it refers to inner balance that supports health. In your career, alignment means your ambition flows in step with your strengths, values, desires, and intuition. You are moving in the right direction in your career and you're experiencing the freedom that goes with it.

I call this *aligned ambition*: a state of lasting fulfillment, confidence, and clarity that comes from following the guidance of your True Self rather than the fear of your success wound. It's the clearest sign that your inner wisdom and your career are finally working in harmony. It's the daily choice to trust the quiet, intuitive wisdom that lives beyond logic. It exists beyond what culture expects, what your family believes is best, and what makes sense to your boss, friends, or colleagues.

Aligned ambition is where our drive meets fulfillment. In its simplest terms, ambition is a strong desire or determination to do something. Whether your dream is to start a business, make it to the C-suite, or start a family, ambition is both a vision for a new future that doesn't exist and the determination to make it a reality. Our ambition is our creative force and our birthright; we have choice in what we mix our labor with, and what is created as a result.

You can't hustle your way to contentment or please your way to confidence. Your ways of working have to also contain the feeling you want the end state to give you. Fulfillment is a state of being, not a destination. Bringing your core states of being (that you set in the previous chapter) into your daily life will allow you to experience more of those feelings now. This is what true career fulfillment is about, aligning the ends (your goals) with the means (your ways of working).

THE FIVE TYPES OF ALIGNED ACHIEVERS

Aligned ambition is what it means to work from your innate strengths. The True Self draws out the gifts within each Unfulfilled Achiever type, turning the liabilities into assets: the Grinder's work ethic, the Pleaser's empathetic leadership, the Seeker's curiosity and initiative, the Hider's hidden desire, and the passion and drive of the Work Hard, Play Hard. The stories below are a snapshot in time of their aligned ambition in action and what's possible for you, too. How they got here—the exact changes they made, and how you can do it, too—is detailed in Part 2.

Grinder

Grinders are no stranger to hard work. When all that work ethic is channeled toward something they actually care about and is used in a sustainable way, they are absolutely unstoppable. Mei, whom we met in Chapter 1, was no exception. She signed into our virtual meeting with a look I hadn't seen before. "How are you?" I asked. "Never better," she replied, exhaling deeply as if she had been holding her breath for days, because she had. She had been preparing for an annual user experience summit with twelve hundred attendees. As a self-described shark without a resting state, for Mei this season of the year was usually fraught with long days, sleepless nights, and little support. But this time had been different.

"This felt like my final exam for my aligned ambition. I was able to put to the test all of the mental, emotional, and behavioral tools I've learned during this busy time. And I have to say, I think I passed the test," she confidently shared. I asked her to walk me through some of those changes and how those shifts showed up in the last few weeks.

Mei learned to channel her diligent work ethic in focused sprints, identifying and tackling key tasks like creating the summit agenda and gaining stakeholder buy-in, then resting for the night. She knew that if her laptop wasn't closed by 10 p.m., she would never make it through the busy season without burning out or snapping at her team. She embraced the idea that she, like an elite race car driver, needed pit stops in order to win. She began building sustainable habits to support her energy. And she was able to stick to them more often than not. Asking herself the question, *How am I best used here?* to practice the disciplined pursuit of *less* (which you can learn about in Chapter 7), she identified where she should allocate her time and attention, and where she needed to outsource help.

"I was *way* more productive and effective in my role, able to accomplish more in less time," Mei reported. "I actually leaned on my team, and I could tell they were a lot more motivated. I used to think if I asked for support, people would think it was because

I couldn't do it. That fear is long gone because I can see that my value comes in my *being*—being present, being strategic, being grounded." Her drive to succeed came from a desire to contribute fully—rather than do it all herself—while taking care of herself. Her ambition was aligned with a bigger vision for herself and her team, allowing her to work smarter and achieve results.

Hider

If I had to pick, I'd say my favorite transformation is when a Hider realizes that the only failure is never giving yourself the chance to try. When worthiness is centered within you, not something you earn, your inner Hider becomes less of a saboteur and more of a guide. It no longer stops you from realizing your potential but helps you move forward in your career with thought and intention. The goal isn't to exile this useful part of you but to integrate it as part of your growth strategy.

That is exactly what happened with Sutton. She was finally ready to break free of the groundhog day that was her life in finance and decided to take uncomfortable yet necessary action. We last saw Sutton after she decided to take a severance package, which gave her six months to figure out what's next while giving herself a much-needed break after over a decade in investment banking.

Maybe for some people, choosing to step off the corporate ladder would be seen as playing small. But for Sutton, whose Hider convinced her that her only safety was found in the stable 9 a.m. to 9 p.m. schedule at the same investment bank, stepping into the unknown was her aligned ambition in action. Sutton's ambition wasn't going anywhere; it was merely being redirected toward what she yearned for now: more space in her schedule, time to heal from burnout, and the opportunity to reassess what's next in her career. And what was next was better than she could have even imagined.

This is what's possible for Hiders. When they take small, consistent steps out of the comfort zone and into the courage zone, they build confidence, capacity, and forward momentum. The fear of failure can become an unexpected compass—quietly pointing toward the very next step you need to take on the path to becoming who you were always meant to be.

Pleaser

There's nothing more powerful than a Pleaser who learns to work *from* love rather than *for* love. Talia once told me that if someone didn't like her, it felt like she might die. As a new director with a team of twelve (all of whom were older than her), she equated likability with being a good boss. She sought out this approval by overextending herself for her team. So it was no small shift when she came into a session one day and shared her new mantra:

I care for people, but I don't carry them.

"I really leaned into that idea this week, and lo and behold, I did *not* die," she said with a laugh. Today, her shade of lipstick was a vibrant fuchsia that highlighted the renewed color in her cheeks. She chose beautiful turquoise earrings that shone against her braids. "If my deepest value is empathy, I need to allow people to have their own experiences, too. That's true empathy. If I ask my associate to do something and I can tell she's annoyed, that's okay. She's allowed to feel that way." I was delighted to hear this. For nine months, we'd been working to strengthen her sense of self, and now she was beginning to lead from it.

Intellectually, Talia knew it was important to tend to her own needs before she leapt to take care of others, but her Pleaser part had been such a strong survival strategy growing up that it took her time to trust that she could lead without being a chameleon. As a devoted older sister, Talia knew love sometimes looked like saying no or setting a boundary. Little by little, she brought that same perspective into work. She used the exact scripts to set boundaries and requests that you're about to learn in Chapter 7. Sometimes the most loving action was delegating even the most important projects so that her team could learn. Sometimes it meant pushing back on clients who had unrealistic expectations.

This new perspective created more empowered decision-making for herself and for her team. It wasn't easy, but Talia learned to let her Pleaser's empathy shape her leadership without losing herself in other people's emotions.

When Pleasers like Talia operate from their authenticity and power, they are able to see the bigger picture, respect the larger goal of the team, and not let small personality issues derail their confidence. And in allowing their compassionate self to lead, they show compassion for themselves. Like Hiders, Pleasers can gain confidence through taking opposite action and realize they are safe and good just as they are.

Seeker

A Seeker's freedom comes from allowing their curiosity to lead instead of their anxiety. Chelsea learned how to look inward for answers to her career questions, rather than anxiously canvassing opinions.

Chelsea fully embraced a core truth of the Seeker: that purpose is a way of being, not a job title. It's one thing to know this intellectually, and another to practice it. She channeled the same drive she once used for job hunting to seek out her authenticity, peace, and inner confidence.

She was able to slow down enough to listen to the pain that was behind the dreaded spiral of *What should I do?* and *Am I in the right job?* She did this by learning a new way of listening to and relating to her Seeker's fears (which you will learn in Chapter 5). From there, self-doubt gave way to self-trust and a faith that as long as she was living as her True Self, the right career path would become clear. Her Seeker's panicked voice started to relax. She began asking herself new questions: *What do I enjoy?* and *What lights me up?*

We explored her zone of genius, which illuminated her specific talents in a new way (which you can also do in Chapter 7). She focused on what she could control, like coming to client meetings with innovative ideas and overdelivering on every digital video spot. Chelsea started to feel more settled. She didn't need a new job or a promotion to feel motivated.

After a few months of fully embracing her version of aligned ambition, Chelsea could finally see the source of her suffering and her freedom. "It's likely I will never settle on one career path, and that's okay. I've become more comfortable with the reality that nothing is perfect. I realize now that my dissatisfaction came from my success wound, not the job itself. It turns out, work is fun when you're good at it." Hearing this was music to my ears. Chelsea knew she still had a long way to go. Her Seeker voice still tempted her into old thought loops, like applying for another degree or pursuing a tech career like her brothers had. But the more she trusted her own desires, the easier it was for her to feel fulfilled in the jobs she had.

Work Hard, Play Hard

There's a different kind of thrill, and a deeper delight, that a Work Hard, Play Hard achiever must discover to step into their aligned ambition. When Joy, CEO of a small insurance company in Texas, made that shift, she was surprised by what she found. Instead of burnout or boredom, she experienced genuine joy and a quiet kind of excitement.

For years, Joy's pattern had been all intensity. She plowed through her to-do list, ran her business with military precision, and collapsed into the weekend with a bottle of chardonnay and a fully stocked fridge. Being oh-so-busy and constantly productive was another way she avoided the lurking pain of not feeling good enough.

It took time, but slowly she became willing to look at what her Work Hard, Play Hard was protecting. She felt the pain of her wounds—growing up in an Irish Catholic home where she hadn't received the validation and recognition she longed for. She began to build a new relationship with this part of herself. Her Work Hard, Play Hard identity wasn't something she had to fight or suppress. It was a part of her that had worked very hard to keep her safe.

"I used to think my problem was weak willpower," Joy told me. "But that explanation never made sense since I'm so controlled in other areas of my life."

Work Hard, Play Hards, like all achievers, have remarkably high willpower and self-control. Once Joy was able to turn down the dial of intensity on her Monday-to-Friday grind, she was able to find a more balanced approach to work. And like so many high achievers, she didn't lack discipline; she had it in spades.

What she needed was genuine satisfaction. Not the quick pleasures found in her nightcap. The genuine, everyday pleasures found through creativity, presence, and intentionality. Instead of treating stillness as weakness, she approached it like a practice. As a result, dormant creative impulses started arising; she began to work with wood she found on the farm, making figurines and eventually a table and chair set for her niece.

"I didn't know there could be so much enjoyment in slowing down and tapping into creativity. It's a much more enriching way to live life," Joy said. Her life began to feel fuller—not because she was doing more, but because she was finally tuned in.

When Work Hard, Play Hards start to look inward for satisfaction and validation instead of chasing external rewards or approval, they are able to experience a newfound elation. The highs may be softer. But the lows stop crashing. They begin to live in a steadier place, where calm is as welcome as excitement.

WORKING FROM YOUR WHOLENESS VERSUS YOUR WOUND

Many people believe fulfillment comes from what you do—your job title, responsibilities, or daily tasks—but real satisfaction comes from where you're working from. Lasting fulfillment is about working from wholeness. Just like the lamp in your living room needs an electrical outlet to illuminate, your ambition is also a conduit that needs a power source. While your house may have multiple outlets, our psyches only have two sources of power: the wholeness and inherent worth of our True Self, or the false inadequacy and crippling fear of our success wound.

Our True Self naturally desires goals and objectives that are most fulfilling. Pursuing intrinsic career goals leads to higher motivation and job satisfaction. I feel engaged with my work when I'm learning a new Excel formula that once intimidated me, or mastering my public speaking skills, or going above and beyond to better serve my clients. You, too, have likely experienced the internal sense of gratification and self-esteem from pursuing goals like this.

Yet I still desire extrinsic goals. I covet wealth, status, and approval from strangers on the internet, despite the fact that research has shown that these types of wants can actually erode confidence and increase anxiety.[1] When I'm shaken out of the illusion, I realize that the part of me that wants *more* is actually a hurt part of me that doesn't believe she is enough. And when I work only to amass *more*, I'm left with less—less energy, less confidence, less creativity, less bravery.

Aligned ambition assumes our worth is inherent and allows us to tap into this power as our source of inspiration, creativity, and growth at work, leading to better well-being outcomes and work performance. Research on high performers who achieve their goals through positive self-talk and a desire to do their best has shown they have greater self-esteem, more confidence, as well as increased work engagement and higher job satisfaction. They are also more likely to take on responsibilities at work and excel in doing so. On the other hand, people who strive toward unrealistically high standards, alongside negative reinforcement and a strong fear of failure and judgment, experience more depression, anxiety, less confidence, and lower work engagement.[2]

WHEN AMBITION TURNS MANIC

Another misconception among high achievers is that determination is the key ingredient to career success and satisfaction. If you can "make things happen," then you'll finally be satisfied. We hear the same message from self-help gurus, or in podcast interviews with the founders of billion-dollar companies: Your dream life is just on the other side of your ability to build it.

But underneath this gospel of determination is a premise of scarcity, an assumption that there's not enough to go around. Wealth and status is a zero-sum game; you need to get yours or someone else will take it. This latent fear permeates our economy and our workplaces. It all manifests in our psyches as our success wounds.

This "make it happen or else" mindset can create the conditions for a manic ambition, a frenzied need to succeed at all costs. Early in my career, I was so fixated on getting promoted that I was in a secret competition with my coworkers in my head. I couldn't be happy for a coworker friend who told me that she hit her sales target early. Instead, her success was my failure. My solution was to buckle down and outwork the competition, which led to more frustration and panic.

At a happy hour, after the rest of the team had gone home, I confessed to a close friend on my team that I lacked a larger sense of why our work mattered. "Do you ever wonder what all this is for?" I asked her over our third beer. She just shrugged and parroted back that we were helping our customers grow their businesses through advertising. And that the salary allowed her to live a comfortable life. This explanation was logical, but didn't help. I felt alone in craving a deeper meaning behind my work. But I finished my beer, buried the question, and kept going.

Manic ambition shows up in Pleasers when they are desperate for approval and to look competent to their colleagues, but they don't actually know what they're working toward. Talia, the director of advertising at a media company, kept volunteering for projects she secretly resented, terrified that saying no would make her look ungrateful or incapable. Her calendar was full, but her work felt hollow.

A Seeker, on the other hand, is like a Ferrari with the parking brake on—full of drive, but unsure where to go. Like Chelsea, who had spent the last eighteen years of her career stuck in cycles of frustration, trying to make something "great" happen in her career but unsure what that greatness could be for her.

With an abundance of drive (*I've got to achieve something*) and an absence of clarity (*What do I actually want?*) and lack of self-worth (*I need to prove my value*), we become frenzied and frantic, racing in circles with no end in sight. Determination without vision leads to frustration (Grinders; Work Hard, Play Hards; and Pleasers). Vision without follow-through leads to stagnation (Hiders and Seekers). Instead, we need to consider aligning our inspiring goals with a more fulfilling approach.

ALIGNED AMBITION IS A STAGE OF ADULT DEVELOPMENT

There's a certain kind of psychological pain that comes from knowing you're holding yourself back in some way, like you have more to express and create, but you fear stepping out into the unknown. For me, this tension between my desire for change and fear of the unknown came in the form of a devastating text message. It was May 2016, about six months after the harassment occurred. I had decided to stop drinking, and for the past three months, I was really struggling without my singular coping mechanism. On this day in May, I had flown across the country for a meeting with a large alcohol brand to discuss their advertising strategy for the upcoming year. After leaving that meeting and walking back to my hotel room, I pulled out my phone and saw that my father, who was battling cancer, had had a stroke and was in the hospital.

Over the last few years, his illness was the backdrop of my manic ambition. My success wound urged me to make him proud before he passed. But this moment highlighted a sharp juxtaposition in my life that I could no longer ignore: I was struggling to get sober while also devoting my precious time and energy to selling alcohol to Americans. *This* was how I was spending my one life while my father was battling for his own? I knew I wanted more in my career than building beer brands online. But I was scared of other people's opinions; what would people think if I left Google? What if I chose the wrong career step and failed? I know now that I wasn't alone in my fears.

Nearly 65 percent of adults report feeling unable to move forward in their lives due to fear of judgment or the pressure to conform. Developmental psychologist Robert Kegan argues that adults go through stages of development in the same way children do. He defines these stages by shifts in consciousness—how we understand ourselves and relate to the world. In his framework, 65 percent of adults stay stuck in a stage of development called the socialized mind, where one's sense of self is heavily influenced by external factors such as relationships, job titles, and societal norms and beliefs about who or what they should be.[3] The socialized mind is what shows up when you stay late at work because your boss's opinion feels more important than your own well-being. It's the voice that says *They'll judge you if you fail* when you consider doing something new, like starting a business or taking a severance package without another job lined up.

The success wound keeps us in the socialized mind by making our value dependent on external validation and social standing. Identity and worth are relational: *I am a good employee. I am a bad mother. I am valuable as you say I am.* According to Kegan, progress beyond this stage requires breaking free from socially defined identity and writing a new one rooted in personal truth rather than social expectation.

This fourth stage of development is called the self-authoring mind, where people see themselves as their own person, defining their identity through their own values over those of their peers or family. A self-authored person sounds like this: *I am me. I decide what's good. I have relationships and I choose who I am, what I do, and what's enough.*

Though it sounds simple, this step is far from easy—only 35 percent of adults reach it. Moving from the success wound to aligned ambition mirrors Kegan's shift from the socialized mind to the self-authoring mind. The former is about social ideas of success; the latter demands an internally guided vision for what's *enough* at work and in life.

For all Unfulfilled Achievers, the only way out is through the very thing we fear the most: carving your own path and risking judgment. Eventually the pain of staying the same becomes greater than the pain of potential failure. Shortly after receiving that text in 2016, I hit my own tipping point. Every part of my being was begging for a break from the hamster wheel of work. Despite the fearful hand-wringing of my success wound telling me it was a mistake, I requested a five-week sabbatical so that I could create the space to listen to my inner voice again. I spent time with my dad. I also spent a lot of time alone, finally being brave enough to witness the feelings I was running from. Taking this sabbatical and getting sober were two radical choices to follow my inner knowing in both my career and my life. Although my success wound flared up almost daily during my sabbatical, this mantra kept me steady:

> *I am me. I make decisions about my life. I define what success looks like.*

YOUR INVITATION

Authoring your own career doesn't mean abandoning everything you've built. Though, sometimes that might be part of the path. More often, it means tuning out the noise of the outside world and tuning into what matters most such as your values, your priorities, and desires for this next chapter. It's about asking yourself: *What do I want to do with this one precious life and how can I do it with my whole self?* Aligned ambition begins as an inner shift. It's the process of moving your identity away from what you do—your job title, your role, your résumé—and rooting it instead in who you are.

This is your invitation into the next stage of your development, away from the part of you that keeps your worth tethered to others' approval.

Simple? Maybe.

Easy? Absolutely not.

That's why most people stay trapped in work identities they've long outgrown, quietly aching for more but too afraid to risk their belonging to try something new.

But you're not most people. You're ready to become the author of your career. You're ready to move forward as an Aligned Achiever, someone who works from self-trust, not self-sacrifice. You're ready to heal the success wound by choosing a new way of feeling, thinking, and leading.

PART 2

HOW TO HEAL THE SUCCESS WOUND

If you were my client, this is the point where we would begin the transition from theory into practice. This is where breakthrough happens. We address the empty-cup feeling at the core of the success wound.

We heal the success wound on three interconnected levels: emotion, thought, and action. Each influences and reinforces the other. Consider the last time you felt overwhelmed or insecure. What thoughts accompanied those feelings? How did they affect your actions? Maybe that overwhelm triggered a Hider thought like *I can't do this*, or a Grinder thought like *I always have to do everything myself.* This feeling creates a perception, which then drives an action like procrastinating or staying up until midnight answering one more email. The cycle goes both ways; our behaviors influence our emotions, too. As you'll learn in Chapter 7, we can act our way into a new way of feeling and thinking that puts behavior at the starting point for change.

These tools are designed for everyday use. They work for you if you work them. Use this section as a guidebook. Come back to the tools when you need to shift your mindset, move through tough emotions, or take an intentional next step. You'll find specific practices for each archetype, but since we all have each of these archetypes within us to some extent, I do recommend reading them all. There's wisdom in every one.

CHAPTER 5

A NEW WAY OF FEELING

Healing the Success Wound Is an Inside Job

When my clients come to me looking to reach the next level of performance at work, they usually ask for "Actions and strategies!" "Best practices!" "Tangible takeaways!" The last thing they want to do is wade into the murky and non-KPI-driven waters of emotions.

Facing the emotional pain of unworthiness is hard for anyone, but especially for Unfulfilled Achievers. It's easier to keep pushing forward in our careers without examining the real source of our suffering. After all, we'd rather be certain than happy, even if that certainty is painful.

No one wants to sit in discomfort. I get it. I'm the same way. I even avoided writing this chapter because I'd rather give you what you're comfortable with in the hope that you continue reading, that you like the book and, by extension, that you like me. But that's just my own success wound talking. I'm here to offer not what you want but what you need to build a career that's not only impressive but also deeply rewarding. By that definition, this might be the most important chapter in the book.

Here's the truth: My clients who experience the biggest breakthroughs in confidence, clarity, and professional self-worth are those who learn to process, regulate, and accept their emotions, even the ugliest or most frightening ones. Why? Because running away from our insecurity deepens it. When we ignore the part of us that's desperate for attention, we perpetuate the very rejection we fear from others. After all, if shaming or guilting ourselves actually worked, it would have by now.

Everything changed when I realized that facing my emotions brought more freedom than avoiding them. A therapist once told me, "Healing happens when we go to the epicenter of the pain and feel it so that it can be released. We do that over and over again, until the emotional pain is no longer the agent of our suffering." She was right.

Over time, the sting of inadequacy softened. I learned to listen to and witness my emotions from a more compassionate place—my True Self. The insecurity that once plagued me daily—the unending self-doubt, the inner belittling, the late nights lying awake in stress—began to give way to a quiet confidence. And eventually, restful sleep. I no longer felt the same compulsion to drink because I no longer needed to escape. I had finally learned to be with my feelings and move through them.

Eventually, I could soothe my success wound's fears in minutes. Before a meeting with senior clients when I'd feel anxiety in my throat or a nervous pit in my stomach, I'd close the conference room door, sit with the sensations, relax them, and return to my usual confidence. This emotional work was the missing piece that allowed my career to finally flourish on my own terms.

The tools for regulating and moving past your success wound are grounded in Internal Family Systems therapy, mindfulness, and somatic (body-based) practices. They come from my own lived experience and from guiding clients through the same process. My story of healing isn't unusual or lucky. It's the direct result of learning how to listen to the emotions that once kept me stuck. And after watching countless clients take these exact steps, I can say that emotional work is essential to career growth.

EMOTIONAL WORK IS CRUCIAL TO YOUR CAREER

Exploring your emotional world is a radical departure from most approaches to professional development. Traditional leadership literature focuses on behaviors like communication skills, time management, or leading through change. But these best practices are hard to sustain unless we address the emotional hesitations that block them. For example, you may know the textbook definition for an *effective feedback framework*. Still, you avoid giving the feedback because of a fear of being judged as too aggressive or demotivating the other person. Even leadership concepts like emotional intelligence focus on the importance of cultivating empathy or self-awareness but rarely teach you *how* to regulate harder emotions like resentment, judgment, and shame.

It's not your ability to get shit done or follow a framework that's missing. It's your ability to connect with your emotional world, because that's where the root of your career challenges lives. Your feelings, thoughts, and actions constantly influence and reinforce one another. If you want lasting change at work, you must examine your emotions and learn to move through them with skill.

Your emotional world is just as alive and dynamic as your outer world. Inside you are many distinct parts, each with their own motivations, values, perspectives, and reactions. Sometimes these parts are at odds with each other. Again, let's say you want to give a colleague some honest feedback that their negative attitude is infecting the rest of the team. There may be a part of you that wants to tell it like it is, knowing it will lead to a better outcome for the whole team. But another part of you, your Pleaser perhaps, fears that it will come off as too harsh. As a result, you let the feedback go unsaid. For the next few days, your mind races with regret (*Should I have said something?*), your chest is tense with anxiety, and there's a sinking feeling in your belly every time this person complains and gossips yet again. You likely won't be able to give the necessary feedback until you examine the fear of judgment or rejection and learn to understand what your Pleaser is trying to protect you from.

Your emotions are always trying to tell you something. They hold essential insights about your needs, desires, and experiences. But we aren't taught how to read and respond to our own emotional cues, so they go ignored. And when you overlook these signals, it is more difficult to obtain not only the career you want but the life you want.

Ignoring our emotions also carries serious health consequences. I can't tell you how many of my clients come to me after suffering stress-related health issues, even heart attacks. Often a by-product of not knowing how to decipher our emotional signals, chronic stress is linked to a range of serious health issues, including high blood pressure and heart disease. Consider the last time you had a prolonged period of work stress and, after it concluded, immediately got sick. The body responds to prolonged stress by releasing hormones like cortisol, which, over time, can wear down your immune system.

Being embodied means staying connected to your emotions and body's sensations. When I was deep in my Work Hard, Play Hard pattern, I was anything but embodied; I was out of my body, living in constant overwhelm. I pushed through migraines and endless exhaustion. My body was an inconvenience that I ignored. It was trying to tell me to find another way to work, but I didn't know how to listen, nor did I want to. My frustration, fear, and self-doubt came out in outbursts like running into phone rooms to cry for "no good reason" or being passive-aggressive to my roommate. It's no wonder alcohol became my easiest tool to blunt my emotions.

IF YOU WANT TO GO BIG, YOU MUST GROW DEEP

If you want to operate at a higher level—whatever that means to you—you must build the capacity to hold the weight of the responsibility, without letting it sink you or burn you out. Carl Jung once stated, "No tree, it is said, can grow to heaven unless its roots reach down to hell."[1] Now, Jung might have been a bit dramatic, but here's how I interpret it: If you want to go big in your career, you must grow deep. Perhaps you aspire to lead a team of hundreds, or to launch and grow a business, or to get better at speaking publicly, or to write a book. To operate at that level requires a grounding within yourself so you're not knocked over or overwhelmed.

My clients fear that if they accept their Hider's anxiety, or their Pleaser's insecurity, then they are conceding to being this way forever. But the only thing they are conceding is the fight against themselves. Confidence comes from witnessing and accepting every part of you—your Protector parts and your Wounded parts—as well as your strengths, values, and interests. As psychologist Carl Rogers once put it, "The curious paradox is that when I accept myself just as I am, then I can change."[2] Change at work begins with accepting the parts of you that are driving the old behavior. As it turns out, we all have the same source of suffering, even if how we cope looks different.

THE ARCHETYPES ARE PROTECTING THE SAME PAIN

We develop a pattern of avoiding our big emotions like fear, anger, or not-enoughness by finding clever ways to suppress them. It's easier to work around our emotions than to face them, especially in our fast-paced world that values productivity and logic over presence. We Grind, Please, Hide, Seek, and Work Hard, Play Hard as a means of proving to the world and to ourselves that we are valuable.

While these archetypes display differing tendencies, they are all working to avoid the same feeling of inadequacy that haunts our daily working lives. Psychologist and Buddhist scholar Tara Brach calls this the "trance of unworthiness." The word *trance* is so accurate, as we get hypnotized into an altered state of consciousness where everything we do, every thought we think, is filtered through our perceived inadequacy.

Modern office culture resembles a trancelike state, going through the day on autopilot, in a daze of stress and busyness, meeting after meeting, living in our automated responses of fight, flight, freeze, or fawn. We are disconnected from our authenticity, our hearts and our bodies, causing us to look up after years—maybe even decades—and wonder where the time went and if we spent it wisely.

To break the trance and to find a more intentional way of working requires you to slow down and feel the pain that you're running from. You likely weren't taught how to actually accept your emotions in order to process them and extract their wisdom (yes, feelings have wisdom). Quite the opposite. In fact, you may have learned that your big emotions (like anger, jealousy, and sadness) were inconvenient or overwhelming to your parents or loved ones, so you pushed these feelings down to maintain attachment and connection. In turn, you learned that having these emotions is "bad" and thus *you* were unworthy of being fully embraced.

Healing the success wound requires us to bravely feel the pain so that it can release. Behind it dwells the confidence, clarity, and wisdom that we are seeking. You can do this through a process called Listen, Witness, Evolve. This method has taught my clients how to finally feel and heal the trance of the success wound and experience the freedom that comes with it.

A NEW WAY OF FEELING: LISTEN, WITNESS, EVOLVE

Just like our physical body has the intelligence to mend a broken bone or send white blood cells to fight an infection, so, too, does our emotional body contain the mechanism to heal our psychological wounds. Listening to our emotions and witnessing the feeling with compassion is like sending white blood cells to our success wound.

To do this, we will use a simple yet effective framework called Listen, Witness, Evolve. This framework is rooted in acceptance and commitment therapy, which helps people become aware of their feelings and to accept these feelings and thoughts to increase emotional agility and capacity for regulation. It's also informed by Internal Family Systems therapy, which I've mentioned is a way to conceive of the psyche in three parts—the Self, the Wounded or exiled parts (where the success wound lives), and Protector parts (of which our Unfulfilled Achiever archetypes are an aspect). The Listen, Witness, Evolve framework is also informed by mindfulness practices, somatic practices, and energy work.

Listen: First, you will practice listening to the Unfulfilled Achiever within. You can do this by locating this part of you within your body, or seeing the part in your mind's eye and asking it a series of powerful questions.

Witness: The stage of witnessing is a transformative process in which you acknowledge and embrace the Wounded parts of yourself with deep compassion. You allow yourself to feel the pain you've been running from without letting it overwhelm you. This allows it to release so that you can access the wisdom of your True Self.

Evolve: Finally, you bring forward the True Self to provide you with guidance, insight, or an action to take next. By bringing your True Self to meet your success wound and your Unfulfilled Achiever, you can restore your True Self as the proper leader of your internal world. From here you can take deliberate action that aligns with your values in the workplace and beyond.

In time, you'll be able to complete these three steps within minutes and the process will be second nature. Until then, it does require practice. At this juncture in a coaching engagement, I set aside two or three sessions with my clients to dive deep into this process so that they can learn how to do it for themselves.

I'll show you how this worked for Chelsea, the account director at a creative agency, who had very strong Seeker behaviors that haunted her for years. At the end of this chapter, I'll give you specific exercises that you can do on your own to turn a moment of insecurity into greater confidence and calm.

LISTEN

When we take the time to listen to our emotions, they reveal our unmet needs and guide us toward healing and understanding. This act of listening fosters a deep intimacy and trust within ourselves, opening the door to wholeness. It's a powerful invitation to explore our inner landscapes with compassion and curiosity, paving the way for a more fulfilled existence.

Most of our working days, we are rushing between meetings and deadlines, caught up in anxiety, leaving us stressed and frazzled. When you're in that state, it narrows your focus and limits your ability to see other ways of reacting or working. When you take a deep breath and bring your mind to focus on the present moment, you can relax enough to feel your emotions. Listening puts us into a state of relaxation in the body. Dr. Herbert Benson's research calls this the relaxation response, and his research has shown that healing emotional wounds can occur when our body is more regulated and our mind is present.[3]

There are three ways to practice listening. The first is by locating the Unfulfilled Achiever Protector in your body and describing the physical sensations that arise when you're in that state. The second step in listening is to check to see if you're relating to this Protector with the compassion of your True Self rather than frustration or judgment. The third step in listening is to ask your Unfulfilled Achiever simple questions to understand its motivations and fears.

Chelsea's Story

This is how Chelsea created a relationship with her inner Seeker that transformed her approach to her career. Chelsea was a born and raised New Yorker. "Well, New Jersey, but only fifteen minutes outside of the city," she said, correcting herself. She moved at the speed of the city, racing from her apartment, to the creative agency's office in TriBeCa, and between client pitches and creative concept meetings. We met at my home office in New York, where Chelsea walked briskly through the door and asked for a glass of water that she gulped down in seconds before plopping onto the couch with a giant exhale. As she yanked the hair tie out of her dark brown curls, I asked her how she was doing, how her day was. She replied with short, one-word answers.

"You don't seem like yourself today. Is everything okay?" I asked. She sighed and said, "I'm not making any progress. I'm still at the agency and have no idea what I should do next. When am I going to get the clarity I need so I can move on with my life?" I could tell this was Chelsea's Seeker speaking, as Seekers live in a state of exasperation. I acknowledged Chelsea's feelings of frustration and pointed out that this was her Seeker talking. "Let's see what else this Seeker has to say. Are you willing to explore this today?" She nodded.

Chelsea was desperate for strategies and practical answers. So when I suggested we close her eyes and relate to her Seeker through her body, she was dubious and told me so. I suggested we view this as an experiment. "Let's see if we can access new data by harvesting it in a different way, starting with the body, not the brain," I replied. She agreed.

Unfulfilled Achievers and our success wound speak to us as physical sensations. For example, I often feel my Grinder as a tension in my temples, and I feel my Pleaser as a tightness in my throat. Other common sensations include feeling a Hider as a tightening or closing around the heart, or feeling a Seeker as the sensation of heaviness in the head. When we tune in to these sensations in the body, we can unlock the feelings and fears of our Unfulfilled Achievers.

I guided Chelsea to close her eyes and take a few deep breaths and bring her focus into her body. We start with listening to the Protector that is most intense or shows up most prominently in our life. For Chelsea, it was her frustrated Seeker. I asked her, "Bring to mind the last time you felt the frantic desperation of your Seeker. Where do you feel this sensation in or around your body?"

"Um, my head?" she said, a little uncertain.

"Inside or on your head? Where exactly?" I asked.

"Kind of in and around my head. It feels like my mind is a blank screen. My whole head feels heavy." I asked her if there were any other sensations she experienced when her Seeker was present. "Fluttering in my stomach that creeps up to my throat," she added. Despite Chelsea's doubts, she was able to describe the blank screen sensation in specific images, giving the feeling in her head a sensation (numb) and weight (heavy).

"If this numb, heavy blankness in your mind were an image, what would it be?" She furrowed her brow and shared, "I can see my Seeker as a girl jumping around, saying, 'What's next? What's next?' over and over. She can't sit still, but she also doesn't know where she's going." Sometimes Protector parts can appear as images, scenes, or personified emotions like a girl jumping around. It's helpful to personify our Protectors because it allows us to engage with this part of us while we stay anchored in our True Self's compassion, curiosity, and courage.

I asked Chelsea how she felt *toward* this jumping girl and the tight panic in her stomach. Did she like having it there, did she resent it, feel neutral, or something else? This is the second step in listening: to check to see if you're relating to this Protector through your True Self or through another part of you. In IFS, this is an important part of connecting to a Protector part—ensuring there's enough Self energy to connect to this part with openness. This allows a container of inner safety to be present instead of judgment or anger.

Chelsea replied, "I hate this feeling. I'm so tired of it. It's been with me my whole life." She said that she was at war with this Seeker part of her and didn't want to give it any more airtime. Without the guardrails of shame, Chelsea feared that her Seeker would take over her life.

Chelsea's response let me know she was not in her Self, but rather another Protector of fear and judgment was present and eclipsing her from listening with compassion. It is common for a feeling of judgment, frustration, anger, or even numbness to step in when examining our Unfulfilled Achiever parts. Just like we need to be listened to with curiosity in order to feel safe and open, so, too, do we need to listen *from* our True Self for our Unfulfilled Achiever parts to feel safe enough to share their motivations, feelings, and experiences.

I encouraged her to invite that frustrated voice to give Chelsea some space. "You could imagine that frustration actually taking a step back from that jumping girl in your mind's eye," I suggested.

"Or you could tell the frustration that you understand its concerns and to kindly give you some space to regard the Seeker feeling with curiosity." She nodded and took a deep breath. "This feels weird, but it worked. The anger and panic is lessened," Chelsea said with a furrowed brow.

Once we are able to locate a place of compassion, curiosity, or courage within ourselves, we can continue listening. The third step in listening is to ask this part clear and simple questions to allow the Unfulfilled Achiever part to share its motivations:

- What do you want me to know?
- What do you achieve by doing your job?
- What are you afraid would happen if you didn't do your job?

As Chelsea closed her eyes and took a deep breath, she centered herself, allowing a space for inquiry. "Seeker, what do you want me to know?" she asked quietly. She put her focus and attention around the jumping girl in her mind's eye. She took my advice to stay present within the experience when her inner critic wanted to come in and judge with thoughts like *Am I doing this right?* She was able to calmly ask this part to step aside just for a few moments. To Chelsea's surprise, after a few moments of breathing and asking the listening for the answer, one came.

She shared, "The Seeker said, 'I want you to know that I won't stop until you find where you belong.'"

I asked her, "Does that make sense to you?"

She pressed her eyebrows together and nodded. "Yeah, it does."

I encouraged her to let that Seeker part know that Chelsea understood what she was saying. Showing these Protector parts that you understand them is part of actively listening to them. It creates trust between these two parts of you.

"Can you ask this jumping girl how she feels about her role?" I asked.

"It's necessary. Someone's got to do it. But the girl is also exhausted and tired from all this searching," Chelsea said, fiddling with a brown curl, her eyes still closed.

I guided her to ask her Seeker the next question. "What is it afraid will happen if it doesn't keep searching so hard?" Sitting on the couch across from me, I saw Chelsea internalize that question and start pulling her thumb ring off and putting it back on. The answer loomed heavy in the air—a success wound that had shaped her self-worth: "I'm scared I won't amount to anything. And that will disappoint my family." This answer caused her to take a deep breath. "Wow, yeah, that's true," she said, a bit surprised with the answer that came.

It was a shadow she had carried throughout her professional life, causing her to bolt and escape to another role or another career idea. Every Unfulfilled Achiever part is working overtime to prevent exactly this fear from becoming reality. That's their mission—protection through overperformance. And they're exhausted from carrying this burden.

"Can you let this Seeker part know that you understand what she's saying?" I suggested. Chelsea agreed. These moments of connection between Chelsea's True Self and her jumping Seeker girl were important in cultivating trust and acceptance. This trust would be essential in the next phase of witnessing the hurt the Seeker was protecting.

I closed the session by encouraging Chelsea to thank this Seeker part for sharing her perspectives and allowing us to listen.

She opened her eyes, took another sip of her water, and asked, "Okay, so what do I do now?" She gathered her hair behind her head in a high bun and looked at me expectantly.

I smiled a little and stood up to walk her to the door. "Well, you've just *done* a lot by learning the skill of listening to yourself. I recommend continuing to practice tuning in to your Seeker part if she comes up this week. Ask her those questions and listen to the answers." I told her that in our next session we would take the next step: witnessing the unfaced and unfelt emotions of her success wound.

WITNESS

To witness the wound is to feel the pain that we've been covering up. This involves welcoming each emotion, greeting it as it arises, and feeling the feeling even for a few minutes. This practice aligns with the principles of Internal Family Systems therapy, where the process of seeing an exile in our mind's eye allows us to witness our more painful emotions. By remaining centered and connected to our True Self, we can navigate the pain without being overwhelmed. We can observe our feelings from a neutral place rather than a critical one.

Witnessing the feeling with openness allows the feeling to release. In her book *Radical Acceptance*, Tara Brach writes that accepting our feelings can lead us to emotional freedom. "The two parts of genuine acceptance—seeing clearly and holding our experience with compassion—are as interdependent as the two wings of a great bird. Together, they enable us to fly and be free."[4]

This process can sometimes bring forward upsetting, even traumatic, memories. While we can be with our feelings on our own, it's always advisable to explore these hurt parts of us with the support of a therapist or trained professional. If at any point this process feels overwhelming, take a pause or move on to the next chapter.

Chelsea Learns to Witness

Witnessing her success wound's pain is what allowed Chelsea to understand the real feeling she was avoiding when she jumped from job to job.

Two weeks later, Chelsea barreled through the door of my apartment like a freight train. "How did the last few weeks go?" I asked. I was curious if she had been able to notice when her Seeker showed up and practice listening to its perspective when it did.

"Some good improvements and some setbacks," she replied. "I noticed my Seeker showed up when I got a passive-aggressive client email and my immediate thought was to quit. I was able to observe my reaction and not buy into it. The anxiety I usually felt dialed down from a nine to about a six, which is great, don't get me wrong. But then I met with two different people, one was an executive producer at a daytime television show, and the other was a freelance marketing consultant. They had impressive careers and they both had different advice for me about what I could do next in mine. The same feelings of confusion and dread rushed back in alongside thoughts of comparison, like they had it all figured out and I never would."

It is completely normal for her success wound to get activated, even after developing a new way of relating to it. After all, these parts have been operating for years, so it may take a while for them to trust her inner leader.

I asked Chelsea if she was willing to witness the feelings that her Seeker has been shielding. She said she was a bit scared but willing to try. I guided her to close her eyes, take some deep breaths, and locate her Seeker in her body again. She felt the heaviness in her head and saw the image of the girl jumping and rushing all over the place. Chelsea noted that she felt more curious about the Seeker than the first time. This was a clue that Chelsea was anchored in her Self.

Next, I prompted Chelsea to ask her Seeker, "What are you afraid would happen if you *did* know what you wanted from your career?" to which her Seeker immediately responded, "If I knew what I wanted, then I would *actually* have to be vulnerable enough to go after it and risk failing. If I don't know, then I have an excuse to stay safely where I am. I can't trust my judgment." Aha. Her Seeker revealed what it was protecting: fear of failure, fear of others' judgment, and vulnerability.

"That's really true. I never thought of it that way before," she said, taking a deep breath, her body relaxed a little more into the couch.

"Can you ask the jumping Seeker to show you what it's protecting? To let you witness the self-doubt, the feeling of being judged?" I asked gently.

"There's just a deep sadness," Chelsea replied, tears beginning to pool at the sides of her eyes.

One way to connect with these big emotions without being overwhelmed by them is to see these feelings within a contained image in your mind's eye. I encouraged Chelsea to do this by asking if she could envision these feelings within a scene or a personified image like with the girl on the move. She replied, "My despair looks like a small girl on a kayak in the middle of the ocean. She's paddling hard but isn't getting anywhere and feels alone. She's sad and alone in her sadness."

This image evoked the pain of Chelsea's success wound: stuck, fearful of falling behind, and unsure where she belonged. These are the very feelings her Seeker had been trying to help her avoid. But now Chelsea was able to bravely witness the feelings rather than push them away. Chelsea was able to stay in her True Self as she saw this image. She understood the feelings of her success wound. This girl on the kayak moved her and tears came.

"How do you feel toward her as you see her there?" I asked.

"A lot of empathy. I just want to give her a hug," she said softly.

"Can you ask the girl if she wants a hug?"

"She does," Chelsea replied.

She imagined giving this hurt part of herself a hug. She held the image, allowing her True Self to send the love, support, and acceptance she'd been aching for. In her mind's eye, Chelsea visualized getting into the kayak and helping the little one paddle safely to shore. This act of connecting with the feeling of stuckness and despair allowed Chelsea to accept the feeling instead of running from it.

Metaphorically and emotionally, Chelsea was back onshore on more stable ground. As the sting of despair faded, and after her tears were wiped from her cheeks, she felt a lightness in her body. There was more space to breathe now that the heaviness had been lifted from her head and stomach. A warm flood of compassion came in to fill the space that the stuckness once occupied. In that space, new guidance and wisdom can enter.

Letting our True Self witness our wounds may be the first time we allow healing to flow through us, rather than trying to control it. In fact, the more we try to control our emotions, the more we stay in the wound. The final stage in cultivating a new way of feeling is to evolve through new insight as the True Self comes forward to lead.

EVOLVE

After cultivating an awareness of our parts' feelings and stories, and witnessing these feelings without judgment, the Evolve phase focuses on applying this awareness through insight and action. Our True Self offers wisdom and guidance that is far greater than your success wound's fear. When we trust this guidance, we open doors to new actions, perspectives, and possibilities that our logical brain can't perceive. In Internal Family Systems therapy, the Self has the capacity to facilitate healing and integration among the various parts of our psyche. From a state of regulation, we can choose how we want to respond instead of automatically reacting from our success wound.

Evolving how we work requires us to consult our True Self as the ultimate source of guidance in our career. To do this, we must learn what our True Self feels like in our body, how she speaks to us, and how to trust her to direct our actions and thinking.

Back to Chelsea

Chelsea had arrived at this phase after bravely listening to and witnessing her Seeker and her Wounded part, represented by the little girl in the boat. From there, she was ready to bring forward the loving wisdom of her True Self.

She exhaled deeply as a wave of calmness and clarity washed over her. It was as if she had stumbled upon a hidden reservoir of energy that had always been within her but obscured by doubt. This feeling—the feeling of presence, certainty, and calmness in her body—was everything she had been looking for through changing jobs.

I asked her to describe what it felt like to inhabit her True Self. "I feel expanded in my chest yet grounded. My mind feels relaxed yet alert, and ready to embrace new possibilities." In Internal Family Systems therapy, this state is called Self Energy. People describe it as lightness in their body—a feeling of being unencumbered. Chelsea's description reminded me of a quote from the Buddha: "Just as we can know the ocean because it always tastes of salt, we can recognize enlightenment because it always tastes of freedom." We can recognize Self Energy because it always tastes like possibility and expansion.

From this space, it's helpful to ask our inner knowing for guidance. I started with the question: *What's there to fear from this space?* I asked gently, hoping to unravel any remnants of hesitation that lingered in her mind.

"Nothing at all," Chelsea replied, her voice steady and light, as if the burdens she once carried had been lifted. At that moment, the weight of her past anxieties just didn't hold the same gravity. I could sense her conviction growing stronger.

"Does it really matter what job you're at, Chelsea?" I probed, curious about her shifted perspective. She let out a laugh, filled with a mixture of relief and realization.

"Not really... it all feels a bit silly from this vantage point. My purpose is so much bigger than a company or a job. My purpose is to be ME in any given situation." To let her energy, skills, and joy lead the way.

"What message does your True Self have for your Seeker?" I asked again. This part of us has the perspective that our Protector Self desperately needs in order to relinquish its need for control.

Chelsea took a few moments to allow the answer to bubble to the surface from her intuition instead of forcing an answer from her logical mind.

"I need to channel my focus away from landing the next job and instead toward what I can do in the present moment. Instead of fixating on the future and constantly asking myself 'What's next in my career?' I need to be asking, 'What's the next right action *now*? What's needed *now*?'"

Chelsea had tapped into the essential mindset shift required of a Seeker: to shift their focus from the fear of the future to what's possible for them in the present.

Emboldened by this understanding, Chelsea committed to calmly and confidently asking herself throughout the workday: *What's needed from me* ***now****?* Instead of fantasizing about leaving her job, she was able to stay present and focus on the work that was in front of her, even when passive-aggressive client emails landed in her inbox. Chelsea was no longer chasing the next job as a means of putting a Band-Aid over her success wound. Little did she know that staying would be the key to her career growth.

When we trust our inner guidance, we open doors that our logical brain can't see. Like in Chelsea's story, you can't fix the problem with the same thinking that created it. Her Seeker had been asking the question: *What's next in my career?* But it wasn't until her True Self suggested a new question of *What's the next right action?* that a new way forward appeared.

We've been referring to this power as your True Self, but it can also be a feeling or concept of love or benevolence, your own concept of God or a higher power, a wise ancestor or guide, or another wise presence. For my client Joy, she embraced the concept of a higher power that looked like a wise guide.

JOY LEARNS TO STOP RUNNING

Joy, the insurance CEO from Texas, embodied a Work Hard, Play Hard approach amid relentless meetings and tight deadlines. She burned the candle at both ends, striving by day and soothing herself with shopping and fine wine on the weekends. Despite her best efforts to comfort herself and relieve the stress, she still felt that sinking emptiness within. By Monday, she was depleted and had little patience for her team and her kids.

In our coaching sessions, she traced her success wound to her cultural and familial upbringing. She grew up in a rural farming town in Oklahoma and was one of five kids. "Hard work was necessary to have a good life. My work ethic is as much a part of my DNA as my red hair," she laughed. Without hard work, she felt lazy, and without a way to reward herself for the hard work, she felt unmotivated. Joy wished for a new way of working that allowed her to be more present with her kids and husband and a less reactive leader to her team.

"But I have to keep working this way because without the stress, it seems everything will fall apart. But at the same time, I can't keep going on this way," she said.

I asked Joy how it felt in her body to say those words.

"What do you mean, how does it feel in my body?" She furrowed her brow. This confusion is typical for women who are so accustomed to living in their head.

"Notice what physical sensations are occurring in your body as you talk about the stuckness you feel in your career. Where do you feel that stuckness?" I asked.

Joy thought for a moment. "I feel a gripping in my throat and a closing in my chest. I feel like my body is constricted and my muscles are tight," Joy replied. I pointed out that this is how her Work

Hard, Play Hard manifests in her body, and reminded her that she's taking directions from this part of her. The fulfillment and peace of mind she wanted was only possible when she took directions from her True Self.

Our True Self is always on the other side of our pain. When we listen to and release our painful feelings, we can access wisdom on the other side. And just like our pain, our wisdom can be felt in the body.

Next, Joy witnessed her emotions and acknowledged the pain of her wounds with compassion. "What if I waste my life by not accomplishing anything?" another voice quietly expressed. Beneath it all, she realized she harbored a fear of disappointing her concept of God. "If God gave me this life, who am I to waste it not working and trying and progressing?" As tears welled up, Joy stayed with the shame instead of running from it. Joy sat with these feelings, witnessing them with compassion as if they were upset children. As the clouds of emotion parted, a warming relief began to shine through.

Finally, we brought in the wise presence of the True Self to give these parts the guidance they needed. "I just want to give these parts of me a hug," she said.

I encouraged her to imagine her True Self embracing her shame and fear with compassion. "How do they react to you being with them this way?" I asked. The tears came again. "They've been waiting so long for me to pay attention," she replied.

"What does your Wounded part need to hear right now?" I asked Joy. "They need to know that it's safe to slow down. It's okay to stop working so hard and living life so fast. In fact, when I slow down I can be more intentional and make better decisions." She was a bit surprised to hear this wisdom come out of her mouth.

"What does it feel like in your body to say that?" I asked her.

Joy felt a newfound spaciousness and softness, melting into her own compassion for the first time. "When I say 'It's safe to slow down,' it feels true. It feels solid and sturdy in my stomach while also feeling spacious and soft in my chest. There's no more tightness or clenching like when my Work Hard, Play Hard feels stuck," she said. Joy realized that sitting with these parts, though uncomfortable, offered her the relief she often sought in a glass of wine.

With practice, Joy could clearly distinguish in her body the gripping feeling of her Work Hard, Play Hard versus the light expansion feeling of her True Self. She discovered that when she followed the lightness in her body, life became easier—and her career began to thrive. From this state of greater emotional regulation and self-awareness, Joy was able to make new choices about how she approached work. It was as if the volume of her Work Hard, Play Hard had turned way down; it was still present at times, nudging her to overbook or take on more. Her next step was to reframe her limiting beliefs.

YOUR TURN

Like Chelsea and Joy, your success wound may be calling out for attention. These steps can be repeated throughout the day as your success wound inevitably pulls you back into its trance. The goal is not to eradicate or push aside this part of us but to develop a trusting relationship with it so that we can love ourselves back to wholeness. After all, peace doesn't arise from a lack of emotion, but from skillfully navigating our feelings. Embracing them instead of suppressing them. Now it's your turn to discover the freedom that comes from feeling.

Healing Exercise: Visualization to Listen, Witness, Evolve

Locate the Protector in Your Body

Close your eyes and settle into a comfortable seated position. Take a few deep, steady breaths, gently drawing your focus inward.

Recall the last time you felt stressed or emotionally activated at work. Who was there? What was happening? Let the feelings surface gently in your body. Focus on your body, not your thoughts. Where do you feel that sensation? Is it in your throat, your chest, or a heaviness on your shoulders? Maybe a pit in your stomach? Does this feeling have a texture or quality to it? Is there an emotion or a set of thoughts that arise when you tune in to this sensation?

You might ask yourself:

- *What sensations arise when I turn inward?*
- *Is there an area of my body that feels especially activated?*
- *Do I notice anything that doesn't fully feel like "me"?*
- *Are there thoughts or emotions tied to this sensation?*

Notice how you feel toward the part.

If you notice anger, frustration, or judgment, another part may be speaking, not your True Self. Ask that part to step aside by asking yourself the question:

- *Am I willing and able to witness my Unfulfilled Achiever through compassion and curiosity?*

Sometimes sadness indicates compassion. Sometimes neutrality indicates calmness. Notice if those feelings are present, which is a sign you're listening from Self.

Ask it a few questions and listen for the answer:

- *What do you want me to know?*

- *What do you achieve by doing your job?*
- *What are you afraid would happen if you didn't do your job?*

Witness your success wound with curiosity and compassion.

Notice if an image arises to hold these emotions. Trust what appears and allow it to remain gently in your mind's eye.

Ask this image what it wants you to know about its experience, about its sadness, confusion, or stuckness. Witness this part's story and let this part of you know that you understand what it's saying.

Evolve through wisdom.

Ask this image if it would feel supported by a gentle gesture—like a hug, holding its hand, or placing an arm around its shoulders.

Ask this part what it needs to hear from a wise, loving voice. Let the words come from your heart.

This might be enough—or you can gently repeat words your part longs to hear:

I'm right here.
You are enough.
I've got you.
I hear you. I understand you.
You're doing great.

Imagine the pain lifting from this part of your body—like a weight being released. Let the shame or hurt gently rise and dissolve.

Notice any shifts—perhaps a softening in your chest, or a sense of lightness in your belly. Feel the calm that follows.

Ask your heart: Is there any wisdom it wants to offer you now? A more loving perspective? A reminder you can return to when a similar challenge arises?

Open your eyes and write down anything that came up for you, including the wisdom gleaned from your True Self at the end.

You can download an audio version of this visualization at www.brooketaylorcoaching.com/book

THE FREEDOM OF FEELING

Wholeness is not cultivated, it's something we reclaim. We are already whole, but we reject and exile the parts of ourselves that we or others have deemed unacceptable. This splintering within is the wound that we have discussed at length. Wholeness is looking at these parts of us and welcoming them back into the fold of our compassion. We witness the trance of unworthiness—the voice that says we're not working hard enough—and we gently reassure it like an upset child. We accept the part of us that craves perfection by appreciating its strength while softening its harsh judgment.

If you want to go big, you have to go deep. Tending to your emotions is the stable ground from which you can grow, create, strive, and lead at your highest capacity. Now, you're ready to create new mental models around redefining your relationship to work and your worth.

CHAPTER 6

A NEW WAY OF THINKING

From Limiting Beliefs to Expansive Possibilities

High achievers possess powerful minds—capable of strategizing, planning, and creating, all while managing long to-do lists and competing priorities. Yet this same mental strength can backfire. Maybe it leads to your overanalyzing critical feedback from your boss, spinning in anxiety about an upcoming presentation, or ruminating on a tough question that stumped you in a meeting last week.

We all carry stories within us that shape how we see ourselves and the world around us. They define what we believe is possible. For many of us, these narratives are anchored in deeply ingrained limiting beliefs. Unlike the seventy thousand fleeting thoughts we have each day,[1] beliefs tied to our self-worth tend to linger and, over time, shape our core identity. Even when our circumstances change, inhibiting beliefs connected to a success wound—such as the belief *I'm not enough*—remain stubbornly intact.

Do any of these negative thoughts sound familiar?

> *I should be able to handle everything on my own.*
> *If I'm not stressed, then I'm not working hard enough.*
> *I have to work harder than my peers to get half the results.*
> *Everyone else has their career figured out except me.*
> *Good leaders don't show doubt or hesitation.*
> *It's too late to change careers.*
> *No one respects me.*
> *I don't belong here.*
> *Things will never change.*

The only way to break free from limiting narratives is to examine them honestly, understand how they shape our emotions and actions, and then consciously rewrite them. By choosing to tell a new, more empowering story, we open ourselves to possibilities that were hidden by our success wounds.

In this chapter, we'll explore how shifting from a mindset of limitation to one of potential can change how we experience work *and* how we experience ourselves. We will examine these stories through one essential question: *Do you want this limiting story to be yours?* Through client examples and practical tools, you'll learn how to reframe your thoughts, break free from old patterns, and create space for a more empowering perspective.

WHAT ARE LIMITING BELIEFS?

Beliefs are the stories we tell ourselves so frequently that they become truth in our minds. They shape how we see ourselves, influence our actions, and determine how we respond to the world around us. And we constantly reinforce them. Our brains are wired to seek evidence that supports what we already believe, otherwise known as confirmation bias.

Each of us carries a unique set of limiting beliefs, often tied to specific Unfulfilled Achiever archetypes. These act like toxic mantras, keeping us stuck in anxiety. These thoughts can also worsen or become more extreme in toxic workplaces when we are confronted with bullying, harassment, lack of inclusion, or other challenging circumstances.

Examining and changing limiting beliefs can feel overwhelming, especially when they've shaped our identity for so long. It's important to approach this process with kindness toward yourself. With time, practice, and patience, those beliefs can be reframed.

Common Limiting Beliefs Across the Unfulfilled Achiever Archetypes:

- **Grinders:** *I have to prove my value by how much I produce and do.* This perception keeps them in cycles of burnout and overwhelm.
- **Hiders:** *If I fail, then I'm a failure.* This fear keeps them from taking risks.
- **Seekers:** *Until I find the right job, I'll never be happy.* This belief keeps them in perpetual dissatisfaction, no matter how much they achieve.

- **Pleasers:** *I'm only as valuable as other people's opinions.* This leads to anxiety and a need for constant approval.
- **Work Hard, Play Hards:** *If I'm not booked and busy, I'm not living.* This mantra leads them to oversubscribing and needing to escape with unhealthy habits.

The key to breaking free is learning to observe these narratives, question their validity, and consciously rewrite them to reflect a more empowering truth. This process can be challenging, as illustrated by Margot's story—a striking example of how the Pleaser-Grinder-Seeker cycle can trap someone in a pattern of overwork and burnout.

MEET MARGOT: THE PLEASER-GRINDER-SEEKER CYCLE

Margot, a thirty-five-year-old lawyer in Chicago, logged into our virtual session with her black hair pulled into a sleek bun. Her nails were always freshly manicured in ballet-slipper pink. Her wardrobe was mostly neutrals—black slacks, cream blouse, with a long gray peacoat—that she called her "work uniform." She appeared to be the definition of put together. She smoothed a stray hair back into her bun as she confessed, "I've quit my last five jobs after only a year and a half each. It's embarrassing how predictable my pattern has become." Why was she leaving jobs so often? Margot told me she would usually get burned out and see no other choice. "I always start off determined to set healthy boundaries, and, at first, I manage to stick to them. But then, when I'm asked to stay late or handle an urgent task, I feel this overwhelming need to say yes, and I give in every time. Slowly, I take on more and more."

Margot's inner Pleaser would start whispering to her that she might get fired otherwise. Her Grinder would echo that she must prove her value to this new group of colleagues by overdelivering past the point of diminishing returns, rereading every contract three or four times. Her thoughts spiraled from overwhelm (*How can they expect one person to do the equivalent of three jobs?*) to resentment (*They don't respect me or my time*), then to frustration (*No one helps me; I get no support*), and finally to defeat (*I should just quit*).

Time and time again, she let that final thought win, quitting her job, only to regret it six months later. As a result, she stalled her career by making many lateral moves instead of upward ones, missed out on significant financial opportunities and promotions, and failed to build relationships that she could leverage because she burned so many bridges in law. Her mind was her own worst enemy.

If you're someone like Margot—someone who experiences higher levels of anxiety and is prone to looping thoughts—you're not alone. Evidence also shows that people with greater levels of anxiety tend to analyze ambiguous events, scenarios, and stimuli in a more negative way, their mind jumping to the more negative interpretation of events.[2] These are called negative thought spirals.

Margot's Negative Thought Spiral

Margot's negative thought spirals stemmed from three limiting beliefs: her Grinder's belief that she needed to work excessively to prove her worth; her Pleaser's belief that she needed to be liked to belong at work; and her Seeker's belief that switching jobs would solve her problems.

Effectively naming the core beliefs of our Unfulfilled Achievers is an essential first step I take with all my clients. In fact, I start all my coaching engagements and workshops with a questionnaire to understand the source of the person's work discontent. Seventy-nine percent of respondents report experiencing a negative thought spiral at least once a week, which affects their ability to regulate emotions and sleep, and make sound decisions. This aligns with research from the American Psychological Association, which found that 75 percent of adults experience stress-induced negative thinking patterns, whereas 30 percent say they worry constantly.[3] While this is a startlingly high number, perhaps it's not surprising when we consider how negative thoughts gain momentum.

Negative thinking often begins with a single thought that triggers a cascade of similar ones, reinforcing a limiting mindset. It's helpful to see a negative thought cycle as the interaction of multiple Unfulfilled Achiever parts creating a cycle of hopelessness and stuckness. You may experience this as looping thoughts, like you're arguing with yourself, or analysis paralysis.

Through my work with Margot, she started to distinguish between the multiple voices within her that were creating a negative spiral. Here's what the Grinder-Pleaser-Seeker cycle sounded like for Margot:

> Voice of the Grinder: *I have so much to do and it's all on me.*
> Voice of the True Self: *It's okay to ask for help or take a break.*
> Voice of the Pleaser: *People won't respect me if I ask for help. I don't want to be a burden.*
> Back to the Grinder: *Law will always be this way, I should just get to work.*
> Finally, the Seeker: *The only way out is to change jobs.*

These parts create a cycle in which the only outcome is the same feelings of stress, anxiety, and frustration. We begin to ruminate in absolutes and universals—*It will always be this way. It will never change. There's no way out.* Black-and-white thinking is a hallmark of being caught in a negative spiral.

Margot needed a cognitive off-ramp from the highway of hopelessness. That off-ramp comes in the form of cognitive reframing, which helps us focus on a more neutral or positive way of seeing ourselves, our value, and our work life.

How Margot Reframed Negative Stories

"So how do I break this cycle? How do I stop letting my mind get the best of me?" Margot asked. I explained to Margot that I use three ways of reframing negative thoughts to find the cognitive off-ramp. These tools are rooted in the work of Byron Katie and her book *Loving What Is: Four Questions That Can Change Your Life*. They also use confirmation bias and the power of visualization. These mental tools are all premised on the idea that events are neutral; we get to choose our perspective on them.

- **Ask Power Questions:** These questions interrupt negative thought spirals and guide you toward a more empowering perspective.
- **Use *Moving Toward* Language:** Shifting from what you don't want to what you do want helps you reframe your goals and unmet needs in a positive way.
- **Visualize from a Higher Perspective:** Creating emotional distance from a challenging situation allows you to gain clarity and develop new insights.

Here's how Margot applied these tools to find a new way of thinking and how you can, too.

TOOL 1: ASK POWER QUESTIONS TO INTERRUPT THOUGHT SPIRALS

Breaking a negative thought cycle begins with asking powerful questions that challenge the validity of your beliefs and shift your focus toward possibility. You can use these questions individually or in succession to interrupt the spiral and introduce a truer perspective.

I started by asking Margot which negative thought was strongest and caused her the most suffering. She identified that it was her Pleaser's thought of *People won't respect me if I ask for help. I don't want to be a burden.* She explained that it was this thought that kept her silent and stuck in resentment. We then took this negative thought through the Power Questions.

Question 1:
Is this thought or belief universally, unequivocally true?

This question comes from the work of Byron Katie, who states that the only cause of suffering is not our thoughts but the fact that we believe our thoughts. She suggests interrupting the thought spiral with the question "Is this true?" because 9.999 times out of 10, the belief is not universally true.[4] The answer to this question can't be *Maybe* or *Sometimes.* For example, is it 100 percent universally true that you're not enough, that you don't belong, that people are out to get you, that you're going to get fired, and that they don't respect you? No, it's not. We have no way of 100 percent knowing any of these things.

"Margot, is your Pleaser's thought 100 percent, unequivocally true?" I asked.

"No, it's not. I cannot know for sure that all people will perceive me to be a burden if I ask for help. I logically know that," she replied. This admission opened up a small window to view a new perspective.

Question 2:
How is this thought affecting my emotions and my behavior? Is this perspective helping me or limiting me?

It's important to see the consequences of our thoughts clearly. We can take our power back once we see the far-reaching impact on our emotions and actions. I asked Margot to pull out a pen and write down all the effects that her Unfulfilled Achiever's thoughts had on her. This is the list she came up with:

When I believe the thought "People won't respect me if I ask for help. I don't want to be a burden," *this is how I feel:*

- Lonely, isolated, disconnected, resentful, frustrated, angry, anxious

This is how I behave when I believe the thought:

- I overwork and lose sleep.
- I lash out at people and get passive-aggressive when they ask me to do things.
- I quit job after job, leaving money and promotions on the table.
- I fail to progress my career in the way that I want to.

Margot was confronted with the expensive cost of choosing to believe these thoughts. By seeing the consequences clearly, she was ready to head to the next question.

Question 3:
Do I want to keep this thought? Or am I ready to see a new perspective?
Again, it's a simple yes or no question. You don't have to get rid of your limiting thoughts; the choice is yours. I've had clients honestly say that they aren't ready to give it up, even if the consequences are severe. They would rather be certain than be happy and that's fine. But when most people see the impact of their false perceptions on paper, they are more than ready for a new one. Margot was ready to see a new perspective.

Question 4:
What's a thought that feels equally true, or even truer, than the original limiting thought?
This question directs your mind to find a more empowering way of perceiving any situation. There's always another way of looking at something, but our brains will only latch on to it if we actually believe it. Therefore, the thought needs to be just as valid as the negative one. You might also find this new thought through asking the more specific questions below to allow you to access your inner wisdom.

- *How would your values respond here? What would (insert value [e.g., integrity, freedom, connection]) say?*
- *What would I tell my best friend or loved one in this situation?*
- *What would a wiser version of me think about this?*

I explained to Margot that we can take advantage of confirmation bias by feeding our brain a new story *so long as we actually believe it to be true.* It's hard to go from "I'm not enough" to "I'm perfect just the way I am" (although that is true!). You may try instead, "In this present moment, I have everything I need," or "I have enough support to get me through this today." Sometimes it can be hard to access self-compassion, which is why it's helpful to tap into your inner guidance or speak to a loved one.

Margot came up with the following thoughts that were as true or truer:

- *Asking for help is a leadership skill.*
- *I can get my career goals met through the support of others.*
- *No one succeeds alone.*

"I feel more relieved just thinking those thoughts. My body feels relaxed," Margot said after seeing these new perspectives.

TOOL 2: USE *MOVING TOWARD* LANGUAGE

Negative thought spirals tend to focus on what you don't want to experience—you don't want to be overwhelmed, fired, disrespected, doubted, rejected. Who does?!

But what *do* you want? This is what I asked Margot: "What are you trying to move toward instead of just moving away from?" This helps to identify the unmet need underneath the sorrow or helplessness. This kind of language helps you reframe goals and unmet needs with clarity. For example...

- *I want clarity on what's expected of me so that I can move forward.*

- *I need more space in my calendar to think about the big picture of where my team is going.*
- *I want to feel more supported by my colleagues.*
- *I need help discerning what's truly important so that I can delegate the rest.*

From there, you can bring your True Self in to help identify the unmet need with compassion. You can then make a request or ask for support in getting that need met. Too often, our thoughts spiral because we don't actually know what our emotions are calling out for. It's our responsibility to identify what we really want and need and to get that want or need met (I give specific instructions on how to identify needs and make requests in the Pleaser section of Chapter 7). That's how you move from being the victim of your thoughts to the creator of your life.

TOOL 3: VISUALIZE A HIGHER PERSPECTIVE

Visualization is a powerful way to see a different perspective. We can create separation between the thoughts and our emotional experience. By closing our eyes and visualizing ourselves stepping outside the confines of this mental spin cycle, we can assess the thought more clearly. I walked Margot through a process to see a higher perspective beyond her Grinder's, Pleaser's, and Seeker's limitations. You can do this, too.

Your Turn: Visualize a Higher Perspective

Close your eyes and take a few deep breaths. Visualize the situation like a scene in front of you. Notice the colors, shapes, sounds, and smells. If it's not a specific event, you might visualize the thought spiral like a thunderstorm or spinning top in front of you.

Imagine you are thousands of feet above the situation, looking down upon it. You are seeing this scene from a broader, more wise perspective.

Look at yourself down there as if she's a character you're watching. See yourself acting from your Pleaser, Seeker, Grinder, or another part. How are you behaving? How are people reacting? Breathe deeply and observe the situation with calm detachment. Notice the colors, sounds, and emotions you feel from this distance.

What does this scene look like from this vantage point? Maybe it seems a bit trivial, less important, maybe even silly.

From this more objective and caring perspective, how would you advise the people in this situation? What compassionate perspectives would you offer them?

Look ahead in time. What will you remember about this a few years from now?

Allow your body to respond to this insight: Let this new perspective flood your mind, relaxing any anxiety in your throat or sadness in your stomach. Notice your body now. Is your throat as tight as it was before? Are your shoulders more relaxed?

Through Margot's visualization, she had a few key insights: "I have so much compassion for the woman who is trying her best to get it all done on her own but who also needs help. She feels so lonely and doesn't want to keep working this way anymore. And she doesn't have to." Margot's True Self wisdom was able to shine through in this moment, and she was able to see a new perspective.

Margot and I continued to work together for another twelve months. During that time, she had to continually return to her mindset tools to maintain a positive and productive mindset. As a result, she was able to collaborate and find common ground with her colleagues and be vulnerable enough to ask for help. "It's remarkable the ripple effect of reframing my negative thoughts. I'm able to sleep better, and even have more compassion for my husband and more patience with my mother. It feels like my quality of life has improved because I know how to see things more clearly now."

Margot was able to counter the negative thoughts driven by her success wound to find the freedom in her perception.

A MINDSET OF EXPANSIVE POSSIBILITIES

The ability to reframe thoughts as they arise and move toward a more empowering way of thinking is a skill that's absolutely critical in your career. Each of us has every Unfulfilled Achiever type within us—certain types show up more strongly in different situations or periods of our career. For example, even if your predominant type is the Seeker, I bet you've had Pleaser thoughts coursing through your mind, like *What do they think of me? Do I belong here?* Or if you're most often a Work Hard, Play Hard, I would venture a guess that you've even had Hider thoughts on occasion, like

Is this really worth the risk? As you read through, I encourage you to embrace the wisdom of each new perspective.

THE GRINDER: OVERCOMING THE NEED TO DO IT ALL

Grinders define their worth through relentless productivity, convinced they must handle everything themselves. This mindset traps them in cycles of exhaustion and anxiety.

Mei's Breakthrough

Mei, a mother of twin boys and the leader of a product team in San Francisco, constantly felt behind. Her Grinder mentality whispered: *I have to do it all myself. No one else will.* After the boys went to sleep, she worked until midnight or later, making sure every piece of code was in on time, and every project plan was moving ahead perfectly.

"It's like I'm a clunky old vacuum," she admitted during one session, "sucking up any and every task in my path, even the ones my team should handle." She was exhausted, anxious, and completely disconnected from the big picture.

Applying the Tool: Map Out the Spiral

I asked Mei to map her thought spiral. Naming the voices helped her create distance:

- **Grinder:** "I have a lot to do, and I have to do it myself."
- **Voice of Relief:** "You could take a break—or quit."
- **Grinder Again:** "No, I'm someone who gets things done."

When asked, "Is this working for you?" Mei paused and admitted, "No, I don't want this anymore." That moment of recognition was her first off-ramp.

Applying the Tool:
Power Questions to Find the Off-Ramp

From there, we reframed her beliefs with new narratives:

- "I have a lot to do, and I'll get it done, one thing at a time."
- "My value comes from being, not doing."
- "It's safe to ask for support."

Saying these aloud, Mei felt an immediate shift. Her racing mind slowed down. She could delegate more, get to bed an hour earlier, and focus more on the strategic priorities for her team. Her mantra became: *My value comes from being, not doing.*

The Six Types of Productivity

One false belief that keeps all Unfulfilled Achievers stuck, especially Grinders, is the belief that there is only one form of productivity. To be "productive" you need to be executing on your to-do list. Influenced by capitalist standards of productivity from the Industrial Revolution, we equate our worth with our output. An essential reframe around productivity is recognizing that there are other forms of productivity that are just as, if not more, valuable. Recognizing that productivity extends beyond traditional tasks, Mei began to see that true value isn't limited to output—it also includes the ways we care for ourselves and others.

Here are the six types of productivity. As you read through this list, consider how you can include these other forms into your definition of what it means to be "a productive person."

1. Traditional Productivity: Writing a report, clearing your inbox, doing laundry, cleaning the house—all fall into this category. This is what we usually think of when we hear the word *productivity*. It includes workplace, personal, and household tasks that land on your to-do list and can be measured by output within a given time frame.
2. Emotional Productivity: This is the time and energy required to understand, process, and regulate your emotions. It includes therapy or coaching sessions, journaling, grieving an ailing parent, or working through the disappointment of another job rejection. When we skip this form of productivity, we risk burnout—not because we're doing too much but because we're carrying too much unprocessed emotion.
3. Restorative Productivity: These are activities and practices aimed at replenishing energy, reducing stress, and promoting recovery. This includes taking a mental health day, going for a walk between meetings, and practicing self-care to maintain long-term efficiency and prevent burnout.
4. Nurturing Productivity: This focuses on dedicated time to care for others: a parent, partner, child, or caretaker. Especially for new parents or for adult children caring for sick parents, it's important to remember how much energy is expended in this type of caregiving.
5. Growth Productivity: Hobbies, workouts, and learning new skills all fall into this category. Many high achievers are naturally drawn to the sense of progress, mastery, and accomplishment that growth productivity offers. But it's important to be present in the learning process itself, rather than constantly chasing the next milestone—the

next personal best, the next Spanish lesson, the next level of yoga.

6. Spiritual Productivity: This involves practices that deepen your sense of purpose, connect you with your values, and nourish the spirit. It might include meditation, reflection, prayer, attending church, a twelve-step recovery meeting, or simply taking time to reflect on the larger meaning of your life. While it's not the same as restorative productivity, spiritual productivity often has a restorative effect, offering clarity, grounding, and a sense of alignment that enhances overall fulfillment.

THE PLEASER: LETTING GO OF THE NEED FOR CONSTANT APPROVAL

Pleasers find their value in being liked and accepted by others. They fear that saying no or setting boundaries will lead to rejection.

Talia's Breakthrough

Talia was the youngest director of advertising her company had ever had. The age difference between herself and her direct peers made her self-conscious. Her Pleaser's default was to help her feel like she belonged in the leadership team by making people like her. Her Pleaser whispered: *I'm only as valuable as other people's opinions of me,* and *If I don't say yes, I'm not meeting expectations.* She took on too much, shielding her team from extra work, and she spiraled into burnout.

Applying the Tool:
Power Questions to Challenge Limiting Beliefs
We used Power Questions to help her challenge that voice:

1. **Is this belief universally true?** "No, it's pretty false."
2. **What would your best friend tell you in this situation?** "My energy is for me. I decide where it goes."
3. **What would your values say?** "I've had empathy all wrong. It's not about carrying everyone's load—it's about caring without over-functioning." Her reframe became: *Care, don't carry.*

Empathy is often a misunderstood concept, especially for women managers and leaders. It's easy to think empathy requires us to take care of other people's emotions, even at the expense of our energy and time. In truth, real empathy gives others the freedom of their emotional experience without trying to control or change it. People pleasing is just the sunny side of control, and Talia was trying to control everyone's perception of her and their experience on her team so that *she* could feel safer. By internalizing these insights, she drew healthier boundaries, delegated more, and found the courage to lead with confidence rather than approval-seeking.

THE HIDER: MOVING TOWARD POSSIBILITY

Hiders stay stuck by convincing themselves they need more time before making a move or that staying put is safer than risking failure. Yet Hiders have dreams of breaking free of this limiting mindset. That was the case for Sutton.

Sutton's Breakthrough

Sutton was on month five of her six-month severance package. She had spent some much-needed time with family back home in Louisiana and caught up on doctor's appointments. She also decided that she wanted to go into freelance consulting instead of going back into another finance job. And that decision both excited and terrified her. She had taken no action toward building her business. Her Hider voice whispered a deceptively gentle lie: *Go easy on yourself. You're not ready yet.*

Applying the Tool:
Power Questions to Reframe Limiting Beliefs

Her core belief—*If I fail, I'm a failure*—kept her paralyzed. We used Power Questions to reframe it. When I asked what might be as true or truer, she answered:

- "I want to be the kind of person who tries."
- "The only real failure is staying stuck."

With that reframe, Sutton felt just enough courage to take her first small step. She began tapping into her future identity, choosing experimentation over fear and momentum over complacency.

Applying the Tool:
Moving Toward *Language*

We created a simple litmus test: *Is this thought moving me toward a new career possibility or is it keeping me stuck?* That question became her compass. It helped her recognize the Hider voice, break the trance, and choose growth instead.

THE SEEKER: FINDING PURPOSE IN THE PRESENT

Seekers believe they'll only be happy once they find their perfect path or purpose. They are constantly comparing their career with those of their friends, past colleagues, and classmates, wondering if other people have it all figured out or are more successful than they are. This leads to constant comparison and dissatisfaction.

Chelsea's Breakthrough

Chelsea had been practicing listening to her emotions rather than running from them. She was able to stay more present in her day-to-day. When her Seeker threatened to step in, she could bring back her True Self's wise words. Instead of asking *What's next?* she would take a deep breath and ask herself, *What's needed now?* This brought her focus back into the present moment, allowing her to tend to her own needs for reassurance that she's on the right path for now and focus on the work in front of her.

"Even though I've made a lot of progress, I can still fall into the trap of believing there's a better career path, and I need to find it before I can be happy," Chelsea shared in one of our sessions. I reassured her that it was normal to have these old thoughts creep back in, and I guided her through a visualization practice to see purpose from a different perspective.

Applying the Tool: Visualization

Chelsea closed her eyes and envisioned herself looking at her career from a ten-thousand-foot view. She saw all the jobs, her choices, missteps, and victories spread out like a winding path. That every job taught her something she still uses today. That every misstep was actually a detour in the right direction.

From a more neutral perspective, Chelsea was able to see that life isn't about finding a perfect path but creating one.

Her reframe: "I'm a creator, not just an employee. My path will grow as I grow." By embracing a creative, flexible approach to her career, Chelsea released the pressure to find a singular purpose and began exploring new possibilities.

Reframing Purpose: The Creative Opportunity

Chelsea and I explored how creativity exists outside the constraints of right and wrong. She learned to view her career as an evolving journey, finding fulfillment in experimentation rather than perfection. When she really grasped this, like all Seekers, she was able to relax and enjoy the creative opportunity in front of her.

Like building sandcastles, creativity is an act of impermanence. We construct, and then, sometimes, see our work washed away. We build products that might get deprioritized or sunset. We build teams and then those people move on. But the point isn't permanence—it's presence. Seekers like Chelsea thrive when they embrace the process itself, rather than chase the perfect result.

WORK HARD, PLAY HARD: REDEFINING SATISFACTION

Work Hard, Play Hards live in extremes—pushing themselves to excel at work while using indulgence as a release valve.

Joy's Breakthrough

Joy, the red-headed CEO from San Antonio, had it all—the company, the farm, the family—except the satisfaction she yearned for. Her belief: "If I'm not booked and busy then I'm not truly living" left her exhausted, anxious and increasingly unfulfilled.

Applying the Tool:

Moving Toward *Language*

We surfaced the core beliefs driving Joy's Work Hard, Play Hard cycle:

- *If I'm not booked and busy, then I'm not truly living.*
- *Satisfaction comes from doing the best and being the best.*
- *Control is safety.*
- *I deserve to relax however I want. I've worked hard for it.*

Next, we applied the tool of *moving toward* language: "What do you want more of?"

Joy paused, then answered:

"Satisfaction that lasts longer than my glass of wine."
"Fulfillment that comes from living in alignment with my values."
"Peace of mind I can hold on to—even when the anxiety comes back."

Joy was able to see what she was *actually* craving. She could also recognize how her Work Hard, Play Hard was actually robbing her of the satisfaction that she so deeply wanted.

Applying the Tool:
A Higher Perspective

I guided Joy to access her inner wisdom by visualizing her life from a higher perspective. This visualization exercise helped her to see how her manic schedule, her drinking, and mindless eating were affecting her with a calm detachment. "It's confronting but eye-opening to watch myself from a ten-thousand-foot view. She looks like she's sprinting with no direction, like a chicken with her head cut off." Then, with clarity: "I need to be more intentional with how I spend my energy. I know I'm driving myself crazy, but I can also see how I'm hurting my family in the process. If I make deliberate choices, I can finally have the fulfillment and peace of mind I've been chasing."

Through these insights and tapping into a wiser perspective, Joy embraced a new definition of satisfaction rooted in self-respect. By identifying what truly mattered—intentionality, peace, and alignment with her values—Joy began making deliberate choices about how she spent her time and energy. She realized that true satisfaction comes from living intentionally, not from external validation.

CULTIVATING A MINDSET OF POSSIBILITY

Our careers change when we shift our mindset from one of limitation to one of possibility. Behind all the mental chatter that you're not doing enough, that you should be working harder, or more, or differently, there's another voice that tells you: *It's all going to be okay.* Past your to-do list, past the mental load you carry to keep the train on the proverbial tracks, there's another softer voice that encourages you to take a deep breath and put one foot in front of the other. Our True Self speaks to us to calm our anxiety and open our hearts. It sees expansive possibilities where the success wound sees only limitations through control. Employing this new way of thinking is crucial for regulating stress and adapting to work demands, and it begins with understanding how negative thinking takes hold of us.

We can access our internal voice of reason through cognitive reframes found in the Power Questions, using *moving toward* language or visualizing from a higher perspective. When we do this, we are able to find a more accurate lens through which to see our worth, our work, and our world.

- Grinders: "I can prove my value by how much I produce and do." → "I have a lot to do, and I'll get it done, one thing at a time." "My value comes from being, not doing."
- Seekers: "Until I find the right job, I'll never be happy." → "I'm a creator, not just an employee. My path can evolve as I do."
- Hiders: "If I fail, then I'm a failure." → "I want to be the kind of person who tries." "The only failure is staying stuck."
- Pleasers: "I'm only as valuable as my last piece of feedback." → "Care, don't carry." "My energy is for me. I decide where it goes."
- Work Hard, Play Hards: "If I'm not booked and busy, I'm not living." → "Satisfaction comes from living in alignment with my values."

I offer these reframes to you to use anytime you find these voices acting up within you. And if these particular reframes don't satisfy, use one of the Power Questions on your own limiting beliefs.

Choosing a more empowering perspective isn't naive or avoidant, nor does it condone a toxic workplace. You may be at a place in your career or life where you feel powerless over what you do for work or who you're working for. But you always have a choice in how you perceive your value and role at work. This is how you move from being a victim to being a creator in your life.

Even if your faith is just 1 percent louder than your fear, that's enough to begin. Because your future isn't determined by your old beliefs. It's shaped by your willingness to believe something new. From this mustard seed of possibility, a new way of working begins to take root, one that leads toward the power, peace, and lasting fulfillment of aligned ambition.

CHAPTER 7

A NEW WAY OF WORKING

Building Confidence Through Action

It's likely that the *way* you work is what's holding you back professionally—not because you aren't trying hard enough, but because you're stuck in patterns that no longer serve you. Many of us have built our careers fueled by behaviors that may have earned us approval or even promotions at the office, like grinding, pleasing, hiding, seeking, or working hard and playing hard. But over time, they've become limiting. They inevitably lead to burnout, anxiety, and dissatisfaction. More importantly, they don't reflect the person you aspire to be.

You're here because you're ready—ready to move beyond the habits of the Unfulfilled Achiever and discover a healthier, more sustainable way of working. But stepping away from familiar patterns, even harmful ones, can feel daunting. You may wonder:

- *Will I lose motivation?*
- *Will the quality of my work suffer?*
- *Will I still be respected?*
- *Could I offend someone and jeopardize my job?*
- *Can I achieve my goals without overworking myself?*

These fears are real, but they are also rooted in the very wounds that keep you tethered to old ways. To be clear, a new way of working isn't about settling for less. Satisfaction comes when you have work habits that honor your worth. By choosing to read this chapter and explore a new path, you've already taken a bold first step. The following pages will show you how every type of Unfulfilled Achiever can let go of unhelpful habits and adopt new ones. Whether it's setting a new boundary with one of the scripts in the Pleaser section or setting only crucial priorities in the Work Hard, Play Hard section, taking intentional actions—small, meaningful changes—can transform your experience of work and build confidence, clarity, and long-term fulfillment.

Embracing this new way of working is a leap of faith from a known present to an unknown future. I've worked with many people who hesitate to release the behaviors of their Unfulfilled Achiever. That inner voice resists change because it fears uncertainty. Embracing change takes courage. You can continue to build your bravery by understanding how intentional actions can shape your experience. Aligned ambition involves reflecting on whether your daily decisions are in the spirit of your core values, priorities, and personal goals.

FULFILLMENT COMES FROM THE *HOW*

Career satisfaction stems more from *how* you work than from what you do for work. I've seen firsthand that when people adopt sustainable habits rooted in their values, their career not only improves—they thrive. You may even find yourself rediscovering joy in a job you once thought you needed to leave. Talia's experience perfectly illustrates this principle.

Talia was ready to quit the career she had spent over a decade building. After a year of working under a manager she described as "micromanaging and erratic," she struggled with rising anxiety and burnout. Her boss pinged her all hours of the day with vague requests like "Look into this" and sent her articles featuring their competitors accompanied by messages such as "We should do this too." Talia's cortisol spiked each time she saw her boss's name appear on her screens.

Talia's Pleaser behavior was in full force—stressing over every deliverable and constantly second-guessing herself to meet her manager's evolving requests and unclear expectations. Her anxiety caused many sleepless nights. "This work environment is wrecking my health. I can't stay here any longer," she said with both resolution and grief.

I suspected Talia's stress had less to do with the job and her manager, and more to do with how she responded to them. Her approach was shaped by a constant fear of disappointing her boss, being seen as incompetent, and a fear of getting fired. I explained that simply changing jobs wouldn't resolve these issues, as patterns like people pleasing tend to follow us wherever we go.

We had worked on Talia's mental loops, reframing her definition of empathy as allowing others to have their own experience. Now, we had to change her working habits that were keeping her stuck, specifically in how she responds to her boss.

She started by making small shifts in her working boundaries. She removed the Slack app from her phone at 8 p.m. She waited to respond to emails that came in after hours until 8 a.m. the next day. She began naming her capacity honestly in meetings, even when it felt uncomfortable. She sought to clarify her boss's expectations from his vague requests. At first, it was terrifying. But gradually, something shifted. She realized the world didn't collapse when she said no. Her team and even her boss respected her.

These small shifts built her confidence to take bigger action. She addressed the communication issues between herself and her manager. Instead of being at his beck and call, she requested that they meet for thirty minutes three times a week so that she could update him and address his concerns face-to-face. She had to remind him of this boundary repeatedly, but eventually it stuck and his anxious, unclear messages were less frequent.

Within three months, Talia's new habits were second nature. Ultimately, she chose to remain in her role, having discovered a renewed sense of confidence and enjoyment. As Talia put it, "I thought being in this role for another year would be a total failure. But instead, the victory has been in changing my relationship with my boss with more proactive communication—something that once seemed insurmountable."

In my coaching practice, 60 percent of those who come seeking a new job end up staying in their role, not because they're lazy or can't find a new job, but because their new ways of working change their *experience* of their job. Talia's story shows how taking action from your True Self can very practically impact your daily work.

How do you know your way of working is on track? Sustainable and fulfilling working behaviors all have this in common:

- They energize rather than drain you, calling on your strengths.
- They align with your values: The action feels like the right thing to do and doesn't go against your morals.
- They allow for the greatest good for everyone involved: yourself, your peers, the business.

THE DOING EFFECT

Confidence is not something you're born with—you can create it. Psychologists have found that our actions can shape our beliefs about ourselves more quickly than changing our thoughts alone.[1] It's what I like to call the Doing Effect. In other words, you can act your way into a new way of thinking faster than you can think your way into a new way of acting. When we engage in a behavior, it reinforces our belief in our ability to change.

Between sessions, my clients commit to specific actions they can take to shift their behavior in the moments that matter most such as sending a weekly impact note to their manager and stakeholders, breaking down a big goal into small daily actions that I call turtle steps, or trimming and editing their long to-do list into essential priorities. They consistently report that this action-based homework is the most effective part of the coaching—it transforms their mood, mindset, and overall work experience. Assigning these tailored actions is one of my favorite tools for fostering real healing and growth.

Staying stuck often leads to overthinking and self-doubt, while even the smallest movement propels us forward, building momentum and strengthening our sense of capability. There's a profound satisfaction in aligning your actions with the person that you aspire to be. Here's why that matters: How we see ourselves and our identity shapes the actions we're willing to take in the first place.

YOUR IDENTITY IMPACTS YOUR BEHAVIOR

Identity is the most powerful force in human personality. The words we put after "I am" influence everything—from the career path we choose, to how we respond when our boss hands us a new deal that's outside our scope, to whether we let it slide when a teammate cancels a meeting last minute for the third time. Here are some examples of identities we take on at work:

- "I'm the 'get shit done' person."
- "I'm a people person."
- "I'm such a perfectionist."

Identity reinforces behavior. For example, if part of your identity is being the "get shit done" person, then anytime someone asks you to cover for a maternity leave, or mentor a new hire, or go above and beyond, you're going to say yes because it matches the image you have for yourself. Your response confirms this "get shit done" identity. This can be both limiting or liberating.

Many of us fall into the trap of borrowing an identity from our career. We may seek job titles or brand-name employers that project qualities we want others to see in us, hoping external validation will fill internal gaps. For example, Sutton hoped her finance career would validate the part of her identity she felt was missing: being seen as intelligent and competent. She said that growing up with undiagnosed ADHD, she always felt behind. "When I tell people that I'm in finance at a top bank, they automatically assume I'm intellectual and hardworking—two qualities I've been trying to be my whole life." Sutton's story aligns with social psychologist Daryl Bem's self perception theory, which posits that people derive their attitudes about themselves from observing their own behavior.[2] Sutton relied upon her finance job to fill that deficiency she saw in herself.

But here's the good news: We can build a new identity for ourselves that reinforces the new behaviors we want to have at work. When Sutton left finance to pursue freelance consulting, she built an identity outside her brand-name employer. She created a new identity statement for herself: *I am someone who is brave enough to bet on myself.* When Talia set a new boundary with her boss, she reinforced this behavior by reminding herself, *I am someone who is confident enough to ask for what she needs.* This is how they created new work habits that changed the trajectory of their careers.

HABIT LOOPS: HOW OUR WAYS OF WORKING BECOME PATTERNS

Just as your identity shapes your actions, your professional habits shape your daily performance. All our Unfulfilled Achiever behaviors fit in this category of habitual action, or a learned response we do automatically. In his book *The Power of Habit*, Charles Duhigg reveals that a staggering 40 percent of our daily actions are not conscious decisions, but habits we've developed over time.[3] In the context of our work lives, this means that nearly half of what we do—from how we prioritize tasks to how we interact with colleagues—is driven by default rather than active choice. To change your behavior, you need to change the habits of your working style.

To understand the impact of these habits on our professional lives, we must delve into the research on how they function. Duhigg outlines how habits are automated responses to cues in our environment that get repeated.

How Habits Work:

1. Cue: the trigger that initiates the behavior.
2. Response: your automated behavioral response, like grinding, pleasing, hiding, seeking, or working hard and playing hard.
3. Reward: the emotional payoff that reinforces the habit.

Let's break down how this pattern played out for Talia.

Talia's Pleaser Habit Loop:

Cue:
Her boss pinging and emailing her with vague requests, like "Look into this," or "We should do this."

Response:
Responded to his pings and emails immediately. Pushed aside other work. Avoided asking him clarifying questions. Walked on eggshells around her boss.

Reward:
A sense of safety and control. Talia believed that staying in her manager's good graces would protect her from being fired—a persistent, though irrational, fear she carried every day.

The Cost of Your Habits

There's one final step that I'll add onto Duhigg's model: identifying the *cost* of your habits. Every negative habit comes with consequences that are critical to name because they help motivate us to change. Consider how these patterns keep you stuck, hold you back, hurt your self-esteem, and affect your health, relationships, and even your finances. The cost of Talia's habit was anxiety, sleepless nights, and almost quitting her job.

Your Habit Loop

Now, let's map out your habit loop so you can see the full cycle laid out clearly. Think about the last time your Unfulfilled Achiever showed up at work. What was happening to trigger that behavior? Map out the habit loop that typically follows that cue below:

Reflection: Map Out Your Habit Loop

1. **Cue:** What triggers your primary Unfulfilled Achiever behavior? Write all of them below:

2. **Response:** How do you typically react? What's your behavior?

3. **Reward:** What immediate benefit do you gain from this behavior?

4. **Cost:** What are the long-term negative consequences? Consider how it keeps you stuck, impacts your mental health, physical health, finances, relationships, etc.

Creating awareness around your habit loop is the first step in changing it. When I first mapped out my Work Hard, Play Hard loop, I wasn't sure if I could change my pattern of overworking during the day and turning to alcohol at night. This way of working felt so normalized and ingrained. Further, my identity relied on this habit; I enjoyed being the person who could deliver great work and also socialize, joke around, and stay out late. Who was I without this? Similarly, you might be wondering, *Well, how else am I supposed to deliver results if I'm not overworking or always saying yes or playing it safe?* That's where keystone habits come in.

Keystone Habits

Now that you've mapped out your habit loop and started noticing the cues and rewards that keep you stuck, the next step is deciding how to shift your response. According to Duhigg, keystone habits are single behaviors that, when adopted, lead to a cascade of positive changes across many other areas of your work and life. For example, if your typical response to a heavy workload is to procrastinate or avoid getting started, then implementing a keystone habit of short, focused work intervals would not only boost your productivity but also lead to better time management, reduced stress, and higher job satisfaction. By replacing your typical response of procrastination with a new keystone habit of short work intervals, you not only change your habit but also enjoy countless other benefits.

Three Steps to Change Your Work Habits

Changing your habitual ways of working can be simple, but it requires intentional and disciplined action. We can start to change the pattern of our response to cues in three steps. These steps are the same ones you'll see in the case studies that follow.

Identify the cue: Pinpoint the situation or trigger that sparks your habitual response. It's important to remember that these cues won't change, but our response can.

Respond with a new keystone habit: Replace your typical response with a new behavior. Below, I will outline specific suggestions for new actions that each type can adopt to have a ripple effect on your career.

Tie your new actions to your identity: If we want to change our behavior, we have to link it to an identity change. Instead of focusing solely on the goals you want to achieve, focus on the person you want to become. Habits should be tied to your identity, making them more meaningful and sustainable. When in doubt, take the opposite action. Ask yourself: *How would the best version of myself respond to this?*

Remember, even a small behavioral change can create a ripple effect throughout your entire working life. Let's explore how my clients have successfully done this.

THE KEYSTONE HABITS FOR EACH UNFULFILLED ACHIEVER

For those of you who have a bias toward action, you're probably feeling relieved and excited to reach this section—*Finally! Just tell me what to do, and I'll do it!*

I've got you covered.

But for those of you for whom action is the hardest thing, this may seem daunting. Here's what I'll say to you: Nothing changes if nothing changes. Period. I want you to look back at your habit loop above. Consider how often these cues pop up. These cues aren't going away. So you can either continue reacting unconsciously or you can change your response.

Now let's bring this to life. In the next section, I'll walk you through each Unfulfilled Achiever type and show you exactly how to identify their self-defeating habits and build new ones that support your aligned ambition.

GRINDERS AND WORK HARD, PLAY HARDS: THE HABIT OF SETTING ESSENTIAL PRIORITIES

Work Hard, Play Hards also have Grinder tendencies at work, aspiring to be the absolute best at everything that they do. These two types have very similar working styles, but what separates them is how they deal with stress and how they spend their free time. Grinders can deal with stress by working *more* and Work Hard, Play Hards numb out to shut their brains off. For this section, I am combining these two types because the suggested actions are the same.

Let's explore the habits that hold these types back and suggest some new ways of working that will help you work smarter, not just harder.

Habits That Hold Grinders and Work Hard, Play Hards Back:

Diminishing Returns

Many Grinders and Work Hard, Play Hards believe that the more they work, the better their results will be. They think that constant effort leads to greater control and reduces the risk of making mistakes or being seen as incompetent. These two types struggle with working past the point of diminishing returns; they can't see the point at which putting in more effort doesn't produce the same level of results it once did. Instead, their habit is to keep plowing through their to-do list, overloading their schedule, and perfecting every last detail.

Mei operates in a fast-paced, hyper-growth start-up environment. She's constantly rushing between meetings, switching tasks, and responding to emails. Research from Stanford University and UC San Francisco has shown that frequent task-switching or heavy multitasking reduces our ability to filter out irrelevant information.[4] This explains why Grinders often miss diminishing returns: Moving constantly between tasks prevents them from noticing when energy or output is slipping. Their hubris around "doing it all" works against efficiency.

Cue:

- A heavy workload

Response:

- Overloading their schedule
- Perfecting every last detail, even the ones that don't matter
- Multitasking
- Rushing between tasks and meetings

Reward: To be seen as the "get shit done" person

Cost: Burnout, exhaustion, anxiety, skipping the gym

Treating Everything as a Priority

A strong work ethic can take you far, but as you advance in your career, the habit of treating everything as a priority can become a major obstacle. This mindset—the belief that everything must be done with haste and excellence—limits your focus and, ultimately, your impact. Early in your career, this approach may be rewarded. However, in more senior roles, it prevents you from thinking strategically and dedicating your energy to what truly matters.

Mei mistakenly believed that good leadership meant treating most tasks as both urgent and important, especially during a product launch. This habit wasn't based on solid management principles; instead, it was fueled by her identity as the "get shit done" person and her fear of failure. Because she lacked clear priorities for herself and her team, every task was treated with equal importance. Without a system to determine what mattered most, she was constantly in reactive mode rather than being proactive.

Cue:

- A product launch
- The time pressure of an urgent deadline

Response:

- Failing to prioritize
- Instead of setting a vision, you're bogged down in the daily tasks
- Putting pressure and urgency on your team
- Micromanaging people's work

Reward: To be seen as the "get shit done" person

Cost: A bad performance review, losing the respect of the team, burning out the team

This was the point at which Mei's manager, the chief product officer, gave her the below-average performance review and said if something didn't change, they would have to find a new role for her. Mei needed a way to prioritize and shift out of her old Grinder identity.

New Actions for Grinders and Work Hard, Play Hards: *Set Essential Priorities*

Grinders and Work Hard, Play Hards are inherently diligent. Their dedication, however, is most effective when channeled toward a few essential priorities where they can have the highest impact. This method not only leads to better results but also allows them to genuinely enjoy their work, fostering a healthy balance and a reliance on collaboration and support from their team.

You achieve more by focusing on fewer objectives. For example, Steve Jobs focused on just one or two key products at a time, and Warren Buffett only invests in industries he deeply understands.

This approach made Mei more productive while lifting her team alongside her. By focusing them on a few key priorities, she shifted her brand from micromanager to strategic leader. Here's how she chose two or three priorities for the quarter and how you can do the same:

Your Turn: Set Your Essential Priorities

1. **Set Your Priorities.**
   - What are three essential, strategic priorities for the business (or organization, or university, team, etc.) in the next three to six months? I like using a three- to six-month time period to address what's most important *now*, and prevent having to switch priorities later in the year.
   - How does my remit intersect these three business priorities? In other words, how does my work specifically contribute to these priorities?
   - What are *my* three most essential priorities that ladder up to the business objectives?
2. **Eliminate Distractions.** Ensure that your energy and attention are directed at these most impactful tasks. This step can be the hardest for Grinders to stick to because the allure of taking on workload is such an ingrained habit. This was the step Mei was falling down on most. Together we developed a filtration system, or a set of questions that she can ask herself when presented with a shiny, new priority that's not on her list.
   - Does it fall under my stated priorities? Yes or No.
   - If not, am I really the best person for this?
   - If I take this on, am I willing to be fully accountable for it?
   - What needs to be deprioritized for this to move to the top of my list?

   If the answer is "No" to any of the above, you can deprioritize or delegate the task to a direct report, or to another team that's better suited.
3. **Ensure Alignment with Your Boss and Your Team.** Present these three priorities for sign-off from your boss. You

might add this to the agenda of your next one-on-one, and ask if they agree that these are the main focus areas. You might also point to other tasks on your plate that fit outside the filtration system above and ask for their support delegating or deprioritizing these.

The most successful people aren't doing the most—they're doing a few essential things with outsized impact. Grinders and Work Hard, Play Hards can work smarter by focusing their energy and teams to extend their impact beyond sheer effort.

A Grinder or Work Hard, Play Hard's New Identity

Finally, they cement this habit by reminding themselves of a new identity.

- *I am a strategic leader who creates outsized impact by focusing on what matters most.*
- *I achieve more by doing less with excellence.*
- *My worth is not in how much I do, but in the clarity and vision I bring.*
- *I am safe to trust my expertise, not just my productivity.*

HIDERS: THE HABIT OF TURTLE STEPS

We all have a Hider within us, a part of us that would rather stay right here, thank you very much, than pursue a dream or a risky *but-what-if?* Hiders avoid risks, preferring the safety of the familiar. However, real growth occurs beyond the comfort zone. Hiders must learn to embrace discomfort by taking small, manageable steps toward their desires.

Habits That Hold Hiders Back:
Staying in the Career Comfort Zone and Avoiding "First Times"

The voice of the Hider tells us that we are better off staying in our comfort zone at work. We convince ourselves that sticking to what we know is the safest, smartest strategy because we would rather be certain than be happy. This is how Sutton's inner Hider tethered her to a career in finance year after year. But this approach couldn't be further from the truth.

Anytime you leave your career comfort zone, you are likely trying something you've never done before. For Sutton, everything about starting a business was new and uncomfortable. I call these moments *first times*. The first time you reach out for a networking coffee or the first time you share about your business online. First times always trigger intense feelings of vulnerability, awkwardness, insecurity, and overwhelm. No wonder she crawled back into her comfort zone and avoided taking action. A first time is a massive cue for a Hider's habit of retreating.

I vividly recall my early days of sharing my coaching business on social media. The vulnerability of self-promotion made me want to throw my phone out the window and hide. I imagined guys from college screenshotting my posts and sending them to each other and saying some version of "She's so lame." This fear kept me from talking about my coaching work publicly for too long. I stayed in my career comfort zone, relying only on word of mouth and referrals for business.

Cue: When confronted with trying something new, such as

- Self-promotion or sharing your work
- Learning or trying a new skill
- Applying for a new job
- Taking on a leadership role
- Starting a podcast
- Sharing on LinkedIn

Response: Retreat back into your comfort zone: say no, pass up the opportunity, keep your hand down, stay in the job, delay the podcast recording, minimize your desires or dreams.

Reward: Feel relieved and safe; avoid the discomfort of trying and failing.

Cost: Comfort kills our career satisfaction, whereas discomfort fuels it. Learning and growth are only possible just outside our comfort zone.

By recognizing that the first time of self-promotion was a cue for my Hider, I was able to create a new response. I shared this story with Sutton, who was delaying getting started on her consulting business. I told her, "You don't have to plunge headfirst out of your comfort zone and into starting a business." Instead, I encouraged her to take turtle steps.

New Actions for Hiders:
Take Turtle Steps

The best way to break out of your comfort zone is through small, tiny, next-right actions. I call these *turtle steps*. Like a baby turtle venturing from the safety of its shell toward the vast ocean, these steps should be small enough not to overwhelm your nervous system. Consistency is key—taking too big of a leap may lead to burnout and avoidance, while small steps done consistently lead to change over time.

Sutton focused on the smallest actions she could take without getting completely overwhelmed. Every day she asked herself, *What is one small step I can take toward my desire of starting my consulting business today?* Over time, this became her new habit.

Sutton's Turtle Steps:

- Monday: Read one chapter in the book on freelance consulting.
- Tuesday: Attend one meeting of the Boston Freelancers meetup group.
- Wednesday: Grab coffee with my former colleague who started her own business.
- Thursday: Reach out to the owner of my yoga studio who needs business strategy support in opening up her next studio.
- Friday: Set up a meeting with my financial planner.
- Saturday: Draft my new LinkedIn summary.
- Sunday: Draft new weekly budget.

This was a huge increase in productivity from last month. She began to gather evidence that she could try without self-sabotaging or quitting. That she could be scared and still move forward.

"This approach has completely changed how I see myself," she said joyfully. Her actions reinforced the mindset shifts she set in the last chapter: *The only failure is in doing nothing.* She also tied her new actions to her identity by reminding herself, *I am someone who tries.*

In one of our final coaching sessions after about eight months of working together, she told me in her light Southern drawl, "I don't know exactly what the future holds, but I trust myself enough to know the path will be made clear. I also know if and when I need to come back to my corporate life that it will be waiting for me." By leaning into discomfort, embracing first times, and taking turtle steps, you too can create a fulfilling and authentic life, free from unnecessary regret.

A Hider's New Identity

- *I am someone who tries.*
- *I am someone who is brave enough to bet on myself.*
- *I am someone who views discomfort as proof of growth.*
- *I am someone who trusts life to meet me when I take a leap of faith.*

PLEASERS: THE HABIT OF PROACTIVE COMMUNICATION

Pleasers operate out of a fear of rejection, abandonment, or judgment. To maintain connection, they prioritize others' needs at the expense of their own. As a result, Pleasers often feel burned out, resentful, and lonely. The keystone habit that all Pleasers need to adapt is proactive communication—learning how to identify and communicate their needs and set boundaries. And, honestly, almost all the types could benefit from this habit!

Let's look at the challenges that Talia and other Pleasers face that hold them back in their careers.

Habits That Hold Pleasers Back:

Avoiding Conflict

Pleasers prioritize harmony and avoid disagreement. They often struggle to recognize their professional value apart from being liked or validated. For Talia, she avoided having a direct conversation with her boss about his management style because she didn't want to anger or offend him. Pleasers like Talia conflate conflict with being mean or unlikable. This pattern of avoiding conflict showed up with her team, too.

Cue:

- Witnessing something that might require feedback
- Group decision-making
- Requesting a raise or promotion

Response: Failing to address important issues directly, pretending to agree with an idea they oppose, suppressing a divergent or differing opinion, failing to address necessary feedback

Reward: Staying in their good graces; being a "good" boss or a "good" report

Cost: Resentment and exhaustion. Not helping the people around her improve by keeping the feedback to herself.

Taking on Extra Work or Responsibilities That Are Out of Scope

Talia was struggling with her habit of fulfilling others' requests at the expense of her own bandwidth. Her fear of inadequacy made her Pleaser come out in full force. When a colleague made a request of her time—to look over their presentation, to mentor a challenging employee—she was in the habit of saying yes. When her boss made vague and urgent requests like "Figure this out," she would push all her other work aside. This was making her not only drained but also resentful.

Cue:

- High-stakes project and deadline
- A request from someone with authority like a boss
- A request from a direct report whose approval they seek

Response: Saying yes when they mean no; taking on additional work that's out of scope when they don't have bandwidth; struggling through a vague request without asking for clarity on the expectation

Reward: Staying in their good graces, winning "brownie points"

Cost: Exhaustion and burnout from oversubscribing. Resentment at feeling taken advantage of.

In his book *Nonviolent Communication*, psychologist Marshall Rosenberg shares the best way to identify our needs and communicate needs to others. He says that whenever we experience an emotional disturbance, it's because we have an unmet need.[5] A need is a universal human requirement that influences our feelings and our behaviors. People pleasing is an attempt to get one's needs met through controlling the other person's experience or perception. I explained this to Talia who replied, "But I still have a need for connection and respect. I don't know how to get that met without doing what they want." Talia's words were profound. She identified the needs for respect and connection that were underneath her habit of pleasing.

New Actions for Pleasers:
Identify and Communicate Your Needs

The first step toward overcoming people pleasing is to be able to identify your own needs in any given moment. It's likely you've never been prompted to pinpoint your needs; this is a new skill that might require some practice! When these needs are met, we feel safe, satisfied, or content. And when they aren't met, we feel resentful, sad, disrespected, dysregulated, and more. My clients find it helpful to have a list of needs to reference when identifying what needs are not being met.

These are common needs at work:

- Autonomy
- Clarity
- Connection
- Collaboration
- Control
- Influence
- Flexibility
- Meaning
- Recognition
- Respect
- Reciprocity
- Trust
- Transparency
- Honesty
- To Be Seen
- To Be Heard
- To Be Understood

Talia identified her primary needs at work as connection and respect. She also had a need for clarity from her boss around his vague requests. "I need my boss to respect my authority as the director of advertising. When he micromanages me, that need isn't being met. I also need clarity around his expectations."

So how do you ask for what you need at work? Here are a few ways to make effective requests:

Need	***Script to Make a Request for Your Need to Be Met***
Clarity	"There's some ambiguity in these directions, and I'm not clear on where to go from here. Would you be willing to tell me what your expectations are here? What does 'done' look like for this task?"
Respect	"I'm noticing a pattern in our interactions. Working well together is really important to me. Going forward would you be willing to . . . [insert requested action: *loop me in on all communication / collate all your requests into an email / give me the feedback directly instead of going to my manager*]?"
Feedback	"I'm really excited about this piece of work. I wanted to share more about my approach and get your feedback around what could be improved."
Trust	"I'm wondering if we can agree on each of our responsibilities going forward so that we can both trust we're working on the right things."
	"I'm noticing a pattern where you're not following through on some action items we agreed upon. I wanted to raise this now because trust in our working relationship is important to me. Can you share more about why this is happening so we can work through it together?"
To Be Heard	"I wasn't sure if I communicated my perspective as clearly as I could have. I want to reiterate it and make sure we're on the same page."

My clients who use these scripts report having much more clarity and confidence in the workplace. Remember, being clear is kind, and we must be clear about our needs and expectations in order to find new ways of working with others from a place of respect and self-worth.

Set and Maintain Boundaries

Setting boundaries allows you to respect your own energy and time, ensuring that you contribute your best work without overcommitting. Common boundary types include:

Time boundaries define how you spend your time and what you prioritize. They protect your schedule from overcommitment, ensuring you have time for your own work and personal life.

- **Example:** Declining an invitation to a meeting without a clear agenda or saying no to a colleague who wants you to take on a task outside your responsibilities.

Emotional boundaries separate your feelings from others'. They protect you from being overwhelmed by the emotions of people around you.

- **Example:** You listen to a colleague's complaint but don't get drawn into their negativity, or you avoid participating in office gossip. Someone might be upset or fired up, but that doesn't mean you have to be, too.

Energetic boundaries are about managing the impact others have on your focus and mental state. They involve protecting your personal energy from being drained by negative or demanding interactions.

- **Example:** You suggest handling an issue over email instead of a long, draining meeting. With a direct report who is demanding a lot from you, you can set boundaries around the topics you discuss or the extent to which you can support.

As I shared these three types of boundaries with Talia, I could sense her rising discomfort. I asked what she was feeling. "I have no idea how I would even start to put up these boundaries. Even the idea of putting up 'a boundary' seems too harsh in a work setting. Everyone is just trying to do their best; I don't want to offend them."

What Talia needed was an example of accessible boundary-setting language. Once I provided a few scripts, her inner Pleaser relaxed. Marshall Rosenberg's research suggests that utilizing scripted responses can reduce anxiety related to conflict and assertiveness, which I'm all for.[6]

Common Boundary Scripts

- "Thanks for thinking of me. I can't do [this request], but I can do [suggested action] instead." *I call this the "No but yes." Saying no to the initial request but suggesting another way you might be able to support or help that works better for you.*
- "Could you share more about what 'good' looks like at the end of this? And where this sits on *your* priority list? I may need your help deprioritizing something else in order to make room." *This works best when a manager delegates a task whose urgency or importance isn't immediately clear.*

It invites a collaborative conversation about priorities and gives them visibility into your current capacity.

Here are some other ways of responding to requests:

- "I'd be happy to help! Would it be possible for me to have [specific resources/support] so I can deliver to your deadline/expectation?"
- "Thanks for thinking of me! For this task, I'm actually not the best person. But [my colleague] might be better suited."
- "This sounds exciting! I'm currently focusing my energy on [specific area/project], so I don't have capacity right now."
- "I can't take this on right now, but I can next week when my bandwidth frees up. Does that work for you?"
- "Going forward, I can answer questions after you've tried to chase down the answer yourself first."

When setting a boundary gets tough, remind yourself of the mindset shifts to support behavioral change (from Chapter 6): *Care, don't carry.* Other people's work or emotions are not your responsibility. What is your responsibility is to fulfill your commitments by allocating your time and energy to how you can best be used. Other people's disappointment is their business, not yours. This is further cemented through a new identity statement.

A New Identity for the Pleaser

- *I am someone who honors my needs and communicates them clearly.*

- *I am someone who is confident enough to ask for what she needs.*
- *I am brave enough to disappoint others instead of disappointing myself.*
- *I am safe to take up space.*

SEEKERS: THE HABIT OF SEEKING TO CONTRIBUTE

Seekers chase external fixes for an internal restlessness. They crave purpose, clarity, and identity from work. But in seeking, they often repeat the same cycles of distraction, avoidance, and dependence on others' opinions. Below are two habits that frequently show up, both in subtle daily behaviors and in major career decisions.

Habits That Hold Seekers Back:

Chasing the Shiny Object

Seekers struggle with trusting their judgment, so they often fall victim to "shiny object syndrome"—opportunities that look sexy and exciting but can never deliver on the full promise that Seekers hope. Examples of this are the false promises from a recruiter dangling a job with better work-life balance when the Glassdoor reviews say otherwise. Or outreach from a past colleague who wants to hire them for a cool new start-up that only pays equity.

Shiny object syndrome holds Seekers back in two ways.

First, they overlook the red flags or warning signs because they are desperate for the shiny object to deliver. They can also put these things on a pedestal, thinking that *this* client will lead to the *next* big client, or *this* goal will finally make them feel accomplished. But when you look more closely, the shiny object is more of an apparition that doesn't fit your values, strengths, priorities, or desires for what will actually make you happy at work.

Second, Seekers get bored or resentful when the job, project, client, or goal fails to meet their sky-high expectations. Ultimately, no job can quell the Seeker's success wound. But they start the cycle anew, as the excitement of a new job or new goals often fades because, once again, they've solved for the promise of the vision, not the content or reality of the job.

Cue: Restlessness or dissatisfaction with their current role

Response: Start fixating on leaving the job; latch on to a shiny new opportunity (job posting, side project, recruiter call) thinking it will fix their career problems

Reward: Temporary thrill of novelty and hope; relief from uncertainty

Cost: Loss of focus, burnout from overcommitment, and repeated disappointment when the shine fades

Decision Avoidance and Canvassing for Opinions

"What do you think I should do?" Seekers solicit advice, direction, and opinions more than other types. When faced with an ambiguous decision or judgment call—whether it's something small like how to respond to a client email or a larger question of what to do next in their career—they panic and freeze. The weight of uncertainty and needing to get it "right" is too much.

Day-to-day, this can look like drafting an email and sending it to three people for review before hitting SEND, asking multiple managers for direction before making a call, or polling friends about every possible next step. On the surface it looks collaborative, but underneath is a deep mistrust of one's own voice. It also comes across as unconfident and hesitant to higher-ups.

Regarding the bigger questions of their career path and future, Seekers over-index on the advice of mentors or experts, thinking someone else has the answer about their perfect career path. Sure, it's important to get advice from trusted sources. But everyone has a different opinion about what the Seeker should do. Often these opinions conflict, which sends them into analysis paralysis. This habit can also manifest in constant comparison as they look at other people on LinkedIn, or other colleagues, and assume that these people have it all figured out.

Cue: An ambiguous problem, an open-ended task, a judgment call at work

Response: Solicit advice, opinions, and comparisons from others

Reward: Temporary relief and validation; sense of doing due diligence

Cost: Confusion from conflicting perspectives, analysis paralysis, dependence on external validation, and a weakened ability to hear their own intuition

New Actions for Seekers:
Seek to Contribute Your "Zone of Genius"

More often what's missing in your career isn't a new boss or more responsibilities. Rather, what's missing is what you are withholding. Instead of focusing on what's lacking or what's a problem or what's next, look within. Ask yourself, *What can I contribute?*

The very best thing you can contribute is your zone of genius. *Zone of genius* is a term coined by Gay Hendricks in *The Big Leap*; it's where your innate strengths and gifts meet the work that brings you the most joy and flow.[7] It's not just what you're good at or what people come to you for; your zone of genius is the work that brings you energy, where you lose track of time and everything feels effortless.

Discovering her zone of genius was a turning point for Chelsea, the account director at a creative agency in New York. We discovered that she is a gifted, creative problem solver. Her colleagues come to her for her outside-the-box thinking on complicated problems—something she hadn't fully trusted but has started to rely on more frequently. She noticed that she felt most energized when bringing clients' visions to life through digital video and that she entered into a focused flow state when editing videos. As she quieted her Seeker's anxiety, she was able to focus on the work that was in front of her at the media agency. She challenged herself to focus on delivering exceptional work *now* without expecting a promotion immediately.

For Seekers, I make this exercise mandatory. Most of my clients do a zone of genius exercise at some point because reflecting on your strengths is esteem-building. After all, don't you tend to enjoy doing the things that you're really good at?

To identify your zone of genius, follow the steps below. My clients find the survey portion particularly illuminating.

Discover Your Zone of Genius

For a digital version of this exercise, including a survey, please visit brooketaylorcoaching.com/book.

1. **Reflect:**
   - Close your eyes, take a few deep breaths, and connect to your heart. Set aside the need to get this "right"—there is no right or wrong here. Consider in this meditation: *What do I most love to do?* After a few moments, open your eyes and write down what comes up.
   - What is it about your work that you enjoy most? What do people come to you for? It doesn't have to be your current job; you can consider past work experiences, too.
   - Write about four times in your life when you were really immersed in a state of flow. Think back to your early life experiences, too. Describe the environment, who was there. Capture the details. Moments of effortless work, fun, feeling at your best. Once you write down the stories, go back and find patterns.
2. **Survey.** Instead of asking others what you should do in your career, ask them what they see as your strengths. Send this survey to ten to fifteen people who can reflect your genius back to you. Make sure it is a cross section of people from different parts of your life: coworkers, employees, a former boss, your parents, siblings, friends, etc. You can create a survey with the questions below or use the link at brooketaylorcoaching.com/book.

- What am I doing or talking about when you experience me the most energized and happy?
- Can you recall one instance when I was at my best in your eyes? What was I doing, and how was I behaving?
- What unique talent or natural gift do you think I bring to my work?
- What qualities or energy tend to fill the room when I walk in?
- Anything else you'd like to share about what you believe to be my strengths or unique assets?

3. **Analyze the pattern:** Collect all the answers and cross-reference to see patterns and trends. Look at your own answers to the questions and see where they appear in other people's answers. Then consider how you uniquely demonstrate this strength. If the theme of "organization" or "empathy" comes up, consider how *only you* demonstrate these strengths to arrive at your zone or zones of genius.

Implement Your Zone of Genius at Work

Prioritize and Protect Your Genius Time: Consider your responsibilities and your schedule. Which of these line up with your zone of genius? Make more time for these tasks by clearing your schedule or getting your boss's buy-in to prioritize these tasks. For Chelsea, this was her creative problem-solving and video-editing time. She asked to only attend essential client and team meetings to free up time to work on her zone of genius tasks.

Make the Shift: Start with small, actionable changes. If your job isn't fully aligned with your zone of genius, look for ways to bring more of your unique strengths to your current role. Can you volunteer for projects that tap into your genius? Can you propose a new workflow or system that uses your unique skills?

Look for the Content Rather than the Frame

If a Seeker does decide to change jobs, they need to solve for the content of the work, not the frame the work comes in. This will help them avoid the trap of the shiny object.

Here's what I mean: Think of any trip you've taken to an art museum. When you look at art in the gallery, was there any piece that jumped out at you? That made you marvel at the beautiful brushstrokes, color choices, or the sheer creativity of the artist's perspective?

Now think back: Do you remember the *frame* the art came in? Do you remember the size of the mat or how the frame was hung? Probably not. But you do remember how the content of the *art* made you feel, how it made you think differently for a moment.

We go to a museum for the art, not its framing. Similarly, we are motivated at work by the interesting problems we solve, the intelligent people we work with, the skills we develop, and the growth we experience. That's our art. The frame that work comes in—the company name, the title, the role, the industry—matters less than the experience of creating and contributing each day.

Before leaping to the next role, reflect on the content of what you want through the questions below. You need to think about the content of the job such as the strengths you wish to hone, the problem you wish to solve, and how you want to feel every day. Then you can fit that vision into a frame (a title or industry).

Your Turn: Finding Your Content

Reflect on these questions to extract the content you're searching for within a job, beyond title or industry or career "path."

- When you look out into the world, what breaks your heart?
- What are the subjects you find yourself drawn to? The things you could talk about or read about for hours?
- What are three things that are intellectually stimulating for you in your work, past and present? What were those problems you were working to solve? And for whom?
- What group or population would you most like to impact through your work?
- How do you want to feel most often at work? What activities or responsibilities generate these feelings for you?

Take a look at the themes from your answers above. What in your answers do you want to be present in your next job or role? Answering these questions is a first step in considering what could be next in your career.

After a few years, I heard that Chelsea had found a new frame for her work art. She was in a new role at a production company that made short films for nonprofits and the United Nations. She enjoyed combining her background in film, her passion for making a human difference, and her zone of genius around creative problem-solving and video creation. When her Seeker voice crept in, questioning whether this job had finally put her on the "right" track, she reminded herself: It met her needs, aligned with her priorities, and allowed her to focus on contribution, not destination.

Trust the 51 Percent Answer

Once you've reflected on your zone of genius and the content of your role, you may still have a few of the same questions: *Do I stay at my job and try to contribute my strengths here? How do I know which path is right for me?* Instead of trying to predict the future, I want you to trust the 51 percent answer, or the answer that's ever so slightly leaning in one direction.

You can do this by tuning in to your body. When you envision the paths before you, which one is tugging you slightly harder toward it? What feels more open and expansive in your body when you imagine the decision? What feels calmer in your body?

The same goes for daily tasks. You don't need to have all the facts to speak up or be completely certain of an answer to act. Learn to trust your expertise and your judgment. If you typically read emails three times before sending them, agonize over written communication, or ask teammates to review your code every single time, then it's time to trust yourself more. Sure, if you're onboarding to a new role, if you are out of your depth and need support, please ask for it. But if you *do* know the answer and need practice trusting your expertise, I want you to experiment with the opposite action: shipping the code after one review, reading your email once and sending it, writing the best response you can and trusting it will be sufficient.

Fear will be a constant companion. Mistakes are inevitable. Self-trust is built through listening to your own judgment and acting on it, even when it feels scary.

A Seeker's New Identity

- *I am someone who trusts my own judgment and inner compass.*
- *I am someone who focuses on their contribution instead of what's lacking.*

YOU CAN TAKE THE NEXT STEP

People regret inaction far more than failure. In my research, I asked Unfulfilled Achievers what it would take for them to finally pursue what they want in their career—to launch a business, work less, prioritize themselves, apply to their dream company, and so on. Many admitted they were waiting for a catalytic event: a layoff, a diagnosis, a death in the family, even winning the lottery. They laughed as they said it, but my heart broke.

Waiting for something external to jolt you into changing is not a strategy. Nothing changes if nothing changes. There will always be triggers—a negligent manager, an egomaniac founder, a high-stakes judgment call. Your power lies in recognizing what you can control: your actions and responses. Start small: Pick one step you can take this week to build a new habit at work. Then take the next one. Progress compounds through deliberate choice, not dramatic events.

Your career shifts because you shift. Now it's time to adjust how you measure that progress. That's where we're going next.

PART 3

A NEW PARADIGM FOR FULFILLMENT

This book could end right now. I could write a nice summary of the tools you've learned and send you back out into the world to practice them. In fact, I almost stopped here.

These tools offer relief, but they are not the whole remedy.

Six months into my aligned ambition experiment, I felt better. I learned to reframe my thoughts from "I'm behind" to "I'm right here" which brought my mind back to the present and toward the next right action in front of me. I stopped overbooking my schedule and slowed down enough to feel my emotions instead of running from them. I uncovered my zone of genius of translating complex themes into digestible learnings through public speaking. I parlayed this talent into a new job at Google where I delivered workshops to marketers and advertisers. Slowly, my life started changing and my career confidence resurfaced.

What I didn't realize was that the culture around me was still pulling me back into its gravitational pull. While my Work Hard, Play Hard was no longer my default, I had unknowingly created another unattainable success ideal that was just as insidious.

CHAPTER 8

LEADING FROM WHOLENESS

Set Your Standards for What's Enough

We exist within a culture that will always tell us there is more to be done and that the work is never over. We need to inoculate ourselves against this belief by setting our *own* standards for what's enough—what is successful and what is worthwhile for each of us as individuals. In this way, aligned ambition is a new model for self-esteem that can be shared. This is what it means to lead from wholeness: to create new criteria to evaluate our labor that centers our worth rather than our wounds.

THE ILLUSION OF PERFECT BALANCE

I remember this exact phase in my own healing journey. Although I had made a lot of progress in healing my success wound, my Protector Self had changed shape. I now sought to be the perfect, balanced worker who could excel without going above a seven out of ten on the stress scale. Wellness became my new obsession.

My days started to look like this: I left my apartment at 6 a.m. for a workout class, followed by a full day of work. I left the office to race downtown to therapy, then back uptown to a twelve-step meeting, followed by a meditation class. I was doing so much work on myself that I felt raw, emotionally exposed, and a bit disoriented. I addressed these feelings in therapy, but didn't share them with my friends. Instead, "Everything's great!" was my canned response to every "How are you?" because I didn't want to break the illusion that I *finally* "had it all together."

One day, I was preparing for a client summit that I was spearheading. We were three days out and I was so scared of slipping back into overwhelm. I judged myself when my old friend, anxiety, started creeping up my stomach and into my throat. I was stressed that I was stressed and pissed that I was overwhelmed. I tried to ask my self-judgment to step aside, but it wouldn't budge.

Once again, I found myself running into an empty phone room to cry at work. Even though I had approached this deadline differently than in the past—setting clear boundaries for myself, delegating, and setting a simple but powerful summit agenda—I still *felt* like I was doing it wrong. *Why do I still feel like I'm failing?* I asked myself.

It turns out I was still applying an unrealistic standard for myself as the "perfect, balanced worker." I thought any sign of struggle was a sign of failure. The illusion of balance is another way we reject a part of ourselves in order to find love and approval. I see this in my clients, too; those who struggle with feelings of inadequacy can fall back into perfectionism, making self-actualization another false idol.

Here's what I realized: If you don't define your own intrinsic criteria for success, your success wound will do it for you. It will hand you an unattainable vision for who or how you should be, which becomes a constant source of comparison and self-judgment.

An aligned ambition statement offers a way out. It becomes a balm to the success wound, replacing unrealistic standards with a vision rooted in your True Self.

BUILDING A NEW STANDARD FOR WHAT'S ENOUGH

During this time, I had a daily practice of sitting in meditation in my New York City apartment and quietly contemplating a prayer from *A Course in Miracles*: "Where would you have me go? What would you have me do? What would you have me say, and to whom?"[1]

These questions are meant to be asked to a power greater than your logical mind—to your True Self, or a divinity or spirit within—whatever you want to call it. Sitting in quiet stillness in my room as the city whirred and whistled around me, I allowed these words to percolate down into my heart and open it, like a tight flower bud slowly blooming. I felt a steadiness rising in my body that straightened my spine and a warm expansion across my chest. I was grounded but expanded, alert yet relaxed. In an answer to these contemplative questions, images came to mind of me walking into the office and seeing the smiles of my colleagues and my clients reflecting back the friendliness and connection that I felt toward myself.

A realization hit me that these workshops and summits with advertising clients weren't just about marketing. They were an opportunity to connect with people from a state of presence. When my success is determined by my presence, I'm no longer looking for approval to fill an empty cup. It's already full.

As long as I was anchored to this intention and showing up as this present, expanded version of me, that was enough.

Through this contemplation and conversation with this power greater than my fear, I was able to create a new, personal definition for success:

I am successful when I rely on the power of my presence and connect with others from my wholeness.

As long as I was working toward *this* goal, everything else would fall into place, even the client summit. I didn't know where my trust in this idea came from, but it felt truer than any other piece of feedback or advice I'd received. Even when I read that sentence today, immediate relief floods my body. *Oh yeah, this is what work is really about.* It feels good and true when I say those words to myself.

At work, my confidence and clarity were able to shine through. While I still cared about how I was perceived by my boss and clients, I no longer obsessed over it. Instead of fixating on being the best at everything, I focused on putting my best foot forward. While I was invested in doing good work, I confidently put my own creative spin on client presentations without worrying if it was right. I intuitively knew how and where to spend my time to have the most impact. Instead of trying to rush my healing, I allowed it to be slow and imperfect by treating my personal and spiritual development as a way to better care for and understand myself rather than to fix myself. I signed up for a coaching course that inspired the career I have today. By allowing my new standard to direct my thinking and my actions, I found myself in a whole new career path I never thought possible.

THE STANDARD CAN CHANGE WITH YOU

And today, my definition of success continues to evolve with me. Now, as a mother and business owner, leading from wholeness looks a little different. I choose to take on thirteen clients and one group coaching program at a time. I reserve another day for inspiring projects, creative thinking, walks, and writing. I spend most Fridays playing with my son and staring at his precious face. I turn down work to protect this space—not because I don't care, but because I care deeply. This rhythm allows me to show up fully energized and focused for my clients while also giving myself the dignity of a more spacious schedule.

It may not look like this forever, but it works for me now. It reflects what I value, how I want to feel, and how I define success in this season of life. I aspire to embrace self-authorship at every phase and stage of my career.

This is what's possible when we set our own expectations and sense of purpose in our work. Every meeting, every deliverable, every deadline becomes an expression of our worthiness rather than a silent plea for the world to validate us. We experience the power in our presence, not just in our productivity. Work becomes an arena for our personal and spiritual growth instead of a constant rat race of egos. With nothing to prove and everything to create, our ambition comes to serve a truer power source. This is the power of an aligned ambition statement.

WHAT IS AN ALIGNED AMBITION STATEMENT?

An aligned ambition statement is a heartfelt reflection of what success means to you, shaped by your inner values and quiet knowing rather than the noise of outside expectations. This statement leaves you feeling satisfied with who you are and what you've done so that you can work without self-judgment or anxiety. It serves as a North Star in your career and your life, guiding your everyday decisions, your career path, your leadership, and how you show up.

When my clients craft their statements in coaching sessions or in larger lectures, the result is always the same: relief, a deep exhale, and a reminder of what matters most. This statement plugs your ambition back into the power source of your True Self, where your authentic strengths are illuminated.

Here are some real examples of aligned ambition statements written by my clients. Soon, I'll have you craft your own, and you may use these statements as inspiration.

Grinder *I am successful when I trust in and rely on the power in my being, not my doing.*
I am successful when I work in a sustainable way that allows me to have longevity in my career.

Hider	*I boldly move in the direction of my desires, pursuing what's right over what's easy.* *I know I'm successful when I am in a state of joy and flow throughout my day and inspire others to do the same. I know these states of being are a choice and I choose to cultivate them no matter the circumstances.*
Seeker	*My purpose is to be myself in every situation. I trust that the right opportunities will come to me from this state.* *I am successful when I seek to contribute to my team, cultivate the growth in others, and learn something every day.*
Pleaser	*It is enough to live in alignment with my values of integrity, respect, and reciprocal connection.* *I am successful when I know my worth is inherent and doesn't need to be earned or proved.*
Work Hard, Play Hard	*I am successful when I allow spaciousness in my schedule and in my mind so that I am present and focused on what matters most.* *My success comes from making intentional decisions to respect my time, my body, and my energy.*

FROM OUTCOMES TO INPUTS

The success wound flares up again when we attempt to control the uncontrollable, such as whether the deal closes, the success of the product launch, our boss's reactions, how a client responds to an email, or our colleagues' emotions. Our success wounds tell us that if we can just get the outcome that we want and arrange everything perfectly, then we'll be happy. Of course, this is a complete illusion that will always set us up for disappointment and resentment.

Instead, we need to flip our focus. A mentor of mine once said, "We aren't in the results business. We are in the show-up-and-do-the-work business." What she meant was if we focus on the inputs—*how* we work, such as our effort, our process, and our strengths—then we've put ourselves in the very best position to deliver good outcomes. The first part of that statement also reminds us to surrender the results. If we control for the right inputs and surrender the outcomes, we can experience more satisfaction with our work while experiencing far less fear and anxiety.

When we are controlling our inputs, we need to ensure they are rooted in the values, strengths, and vision of our True Self. Our aim becomes working in a way that centers our confidence, creativity, growth, joy, and flow *more often than not*. It isn't always easy or possible to work entirely from this state, and that's okay. It's a direction, not a destination.

So what goes in your statement? Aligned ambition statements incorporate six key tenets (or inputs): trust, core states of being, values, zone of genius, growth, and meaning and service. While coaching people through this process, I asked them to consider what motivates them, what they want to contribute to, and the governing principles by which they want to guide their career. The same six principles show up over and over.

THE SIX TENETS OF ALIGNED AMBITION

1. **Trust:** If change is the only constant in our lives, then uncertainty is also inevitable. In the face of uncertainty, we have two choices: trust the flow of life or push against it. We know what pushing against life looks like: micromanaging others, obsessing over outcomes, sending passive-aggressive emails, or shutting down and giving up. Trust brings us back into a state of regulation where our agency lies.

   Trust is foundational in navigating work and life's complexities. It involves having faith in your intuition, the guidance of your True Self, or in a higher power. It means taking action even amid uncertainty, learning to lean into the "51 percent answer" when you're unsure—that slight feeling of knowing or direction when faced with difficult choices. In the context of aligned ambition, it means letting go of the need to micromanage outcomes, such as how others perceive your work or the results of a project. You free yourself to focus on what you can influence: your effort, your intention, your creativity.

   Trust encourages you to embrace the vulnerability in learning, allowing for the possibility of making decisions that resonate deeply with your core self, even when the outcomes are unclear. By cultivating self-trust and trust with life around you, you open yourself up to opportunities and outcomes that align more closely with your true desires.

2. **Core States of Being:** Success is a feeling, not a destination. When we pursue goals, what we are actually desiring is the feeling that comes with achievement, such as satisfaction, pride, recognition, or connection. Rather than waiting for that feeling

as an external reward, you can begin to cultivate it in the present. You don't have to hope for praise from your boss. The satisfaction, pride, fulfillment, joy, or relief can be experienced now. We explored how to cultivate and bring core states of being into your day in Chapter 3.

3. **Values:** Your values are beliefs, characteristics, and qualities that you hold most dear. They guide your choices and behavior back toward your innate sense of confidence. When your actions are in harmony with your values, you experience a greater sense of purpose and flow. Most aligned ambition statements center one or more core values. The instructions to set your core values are in Chapter 3.
4. **Growth:** It's incredibly motivating to feel a sense of progress at work or mastering a skill. Growth allows us to perceive mistakes or setbacks as learning opportunities. It's critical to celebrate *all* progress, regardless of the size or the speed. Otherwise, you can fall into the same trap I did of being obsessed with *more* growth, *more* mastery, and inadvertently make growth another measuring stick for your worth.
5. **Zone of Genius:** Using your zone of genius—the strengths you do uniquely well—puts you into a state of flow at work. We are naturally more efficient and joyful when we use our talents. It's fun to use our gifts in service of a mission or work we care about. Deliberately choosing a role or responsibilities that require your zone of genius is like a turbocharger for your career. When you measure your success by how often you use your talents, you will have an incredibly rewarding and motivating career. You can determine your zone of genius in the Seeker section of Chapter 7.

6. **Meaning:** Finding meaning in your work is essential for long-term fulfillment. Your work doesn't have to be altruistic or world-changing. Rather, it's about finding the emotional thread in your work that moves you. For example, my client Talia, who is a director of advertising, finds meaning in telling a brand's story in digital video. Service fosters a sense of belonging and shared mission, anchoring your ambitions in a foundation of empathy and commitment to making a difference. This is where Mei finds meaning: in leading a team and making products that people actually use.

These six qualities are not just lofty ideals but practical guides for crafting a fulfilling, purpose-driven life. When you prioritize these inputs, you shift your focus away from the fickle nature of external validation and instead root yourself in an abiding sense of inner fulfillment.

FINDING YOUR NORTH STAR

Throughout history, Polynesian navigators demonstrated remarkable wayfinding skills as they traversed the Pacific Ocean. Their navigation relied on a sophisticated understanding of celestial bodies and oceanic currents. They steered their ships across vast, uncharted waters using the North Star as a steady reference point. In your career, your aligned ambition statement is your very own North Star, providing an unchanging anchor throughout your journey. Your intuition, values, and zone of genius are your tools to steer you in the right direction.

Modern research echoes this ancient principle, showing that having a clear, guiding purpose is just as essential today as it was on the open seas. Angela Duckworth is a professor of psychology at the University of Pennsylvania who studies grit. Grit, she says, is the combination of passion and perseverance that allows people to keep going toward long-term goals, even when faced with challenges or setbacks. Her research suggests that the most gritty people are those who have a hierarchy of goals, where broader, long-term goals (or what she calls *ultimate concerns*) guide shorter-term objectives.[2]

A clear ultimate concern creates alignment between daily actions and an overarching purpose, which helps maintain motivation and focus over time. The most gritty people, Duckworth says, are those who are able to pursue their ultimate concern over long periods. It is enduring grit, not talent, that determines people's long-term success. Duckworth emphasizes the importance of these ultimate concerns in sustaining effort and resilience, as they provide a sense of meaning and direction in one's life and career.

Your aligned ambition statement is your ultimate concern; it opens up new opportunities for you. In my own life, my ultimate concern was *I am successful when I rely on the power of my presence and connect with others from this place.* The more I focused on cultivating the energy of my confidence and how I showed up, the more confident I felt.

This ultimate concern reshaped every other area of my life. All my daily actions came to serve this top-line goal. I stopped drinking because it depleted my presence and energy. I showed up more authentically on dates and spoke openly about my interests that I once kept secret, like my fascination with personal development and spirituality. This ultimate concern also influenced my leadership approach at work. I started using my learned coaching skills with my other team members. We set our own team values and mission statement, creating a positive microculture within the larger macro-culture, which could at times feel unmotivating.

You know you're living and working from your aligned ambition statement when you are clear on your intention for each choice. You know why you're in *this* job and why it matters *to you*. Your daily habits (like how you sleep, eat, socialize, where you spend your time, and how you treat others) are all a reflection of this higher purpose. As a manager or leader, you have a clear vision for your team that's a reflection of both the business objectives and the culture that you want to build. Eventually, your whole life reverberates with a quiet hum of purpose and meaning. Our career growth is a natural consequence of this larger spiritual evolution.

With your aligned ambition statement as your ultimate concern, you can't help but feel clear on where you're going, motivated to get there, certain on why your work matters. There's nothing more esteem-building than that.

INTRINSIC MOTIVATION IN THE WORKPLACE: THE KEY TO FULFILLMENT AND SUCCESS

In my corporate group coaching programs, especially in hyper-competitive organizations (like tech, finance, and consulting), participants doubt that solving for these inputs will actually lead to better results. I hear questions like "What good will *trust* or *meaning* do for me when I have to get a CEO on board with laying people off?" or "Sometimes you just have to work really hard and push and influence others to get the best outcome." Their concern is logical, but it ignores some simple facts about human motivation.

These six tenets are forms of intrinsic motivation. Too often our behavior at work comes from motivators that sound like "if… then" rewards. *If you get the CEO on board, then you'll get praise from your boss.* Or, *If you close the deal, then you'll hit your bonus.* But there are real limits in this way of thinking. In his book *Drive: The Surprising Truth About What Motivates Us*, author Daniel Pink says intrinsic motivation outperforms extrinsic motivation when it comes to innovation, productivity, engagement, workplace satisfaction, and longevity in the role. When we identify our own reason for why our work matters and connect with a sense of pride and rewards from within, we are more likely to persevere through challenges, feel more satisfied and engaged at work, and have better performance. This happened to Margot, who was able to tap into a whole new sense of meaning and excitement around her career that unlocked new opportunities at work.

Living Your Aligned Ambition: Margot's Story

Without intrinsic motivation in our careers, we tend to slip back into working from our success wound. This had been the case for my client Margot, the thirty-five-year-old lawyer in Chicago whom we met in Chapter 6. We had worked together closely that year, helping her to redirect the negative thought spiral that had caused her to leave her last five jobs at five different law firms and corporations. While she had made significant progress in managing her rumination, her underlying success ideal remained: *If I'm not the best, I'm the worst.* She still held herself to a sky-high standard and assumed everyone else did, too.

In a virtual session on a Thursday afternoon, I asked her, "How has this week been?"

She sighed, stuck her left arm straight out in front of her, her gold bangles jingling, and said, "Trying to close my laptop at a reasonable time and reframe my thoughts feels like I'm holding a two-pound weight in front of me." She said that the gravity of the prevailing corporate culture was making holding on to her aligned ambition difficult. "I see my colleagues working harder and think I should be too, because I can't let them surpass me or bill more hours than me. I slip back into my Grinder when I'm up all night obsessing about everything I have to do in the morning. I even got out of bed at 2 a.m. because if I wasn't sleeping, I might as well get some contracts done." She let her arm drop for effect. She asked, "Is it even possible to work in a new way? Or will I always just slip back into old habits?"

Margot's questions were poignant and ushered in the next stage of her journey toward aligned ambition: setting a new standard for herself that could serve as her own microculture within the macro organization.

First, we looked back at the values exercise she completed. Her core values were honesty, integrity, discipline, connection, and respect. I guided her to close her eyes, and envision fully embodying these values at work and to describe what she saw.

"I can see myself focusing more on how I can help my clients rather than fixating on billable hours," she replied. "I can see myself being more respectful of my own body's needs by eating lunch, working out even twice a week, and sleeping better. My goal is now working sustainably and smarter so that I *can* stay in law long-term. The noise of office politics dies down, and I can focus on what's most important. I feel an immediate relaxing and opening in my body." This was in stark contrast to her success wound's standard of needing approval and praise to know she was doing a good job.

Next, we examined her sense of meaning and service to her clients: "I'm here to do this job which is to serve my clients well and take care of myself, which leads to a greater sense of meaning," she explained. This was a very different motive than her success wound's desire to be the best at all costs.

Finally, we looked at her ability to trust herself. "When I'm trusting myself and trusting life, I am able to set boundaries and not go back on them. I don't doubt myself," she said.

The rest of the aligned ambition tenets didn't ring as true to her as these three; often people are naturally drawn to, or more motivated by, a few select tenets rather than all six. We played around with a few different versions before landing on this aligned ambition statement that brought a big smile and excitement in her dark brown eyes:

> *I am successful when I am working in a sustainable way that shows respect for myself and allows me to serve my clients.*

"That's totally it," Margot said with a nod. "That just *feels* true."

Two weeks later, I asked Margot about how her new standards for success had influenced her that week. She smiled and said she repeated the statement to herself anytime she felt the pull to take on more work or work past 11 p.m.

Additionally, rather than obsessing about her standing with her boss, she solved for the inputs for her work. "I had a difficult conversation with my boss to advocate for more resources for a client. I showed up with my values of honesty and integrity. I advocated for myself and the client, and asked for what we needed. He blew me off and didn't react very well. That used to send me spiraling for weeks. But I just reminded myself *I am successful when I am working in a sustainable way that shows respect for myself and allows me to serve my clients*, which is exactly what I did in this situation. My actions were totally aligned to my definition of success. I wish he reacted differently, but I don't second-guess my approach." With this intention as her North Star, Margot's ways of working completely realigned to serve this goal.

A year and a half later, I caught up with Margot when I was in Chicago for a conference. She walked through the door of a quaint coffee shop in the West Loop with her signature sleek bun, ballet-slipper-pink nails, and gray peacoat. We embraced and I couldn't wait to hear what she had been up to and if her aligned ambition statement continued to guide her life. She was still at the same firm; it was the longest she'd been able to stay somewhere without quitting in frustration. In fact, her mentor said she was close to making partner. That wasn't the only big change in her life. She'd also ended up having a baby girl. "I never thought kids were on the table for me. But I finally have enough space in my mind and in my heart to have one, and I'm so grateful." While this outcome isn't the same for everyone, Margot was able to find her aligned ambition, which led to her discovering a more whole definition of success that ran through her entire life.

Write Your Aligned Ambition Statement

Crafting your aligned ambition statement is as much an art as it is a process. Below are the steps I recommend to write yours. Take time with this, refine it, and come back to it to ensure it feels resonant in your body.

You may start your statement with any of the following:

I am successful when...
I am enough when...
It is enough when...
My definition of success is...

There's no wrong way to begin—as long as your statement clearly reflects your new standard for enoughness.

Then consider the six tenets of aligned ambition and how each is a critical input that you want to solve for.

1. Trust
2. Core states of being
3. Values
4. Zone of genius
5. Growth
6. Meaning

Which tenets are most motivating and persuasive for you? For example, if your success wound most often tells you that you're not smart or capable enough, consider using elements of your zone of genius and values to reframe how you see your intelligence.

I suggest using anywhere from one to three tenets in your statement. This can take some clever wordsmithing or iteration to find the language that feels most true to you.

This isn't just a mental exercise—it's a felt one. When you have a draft of your statement, say it out loud and close your eyes. Really take in the meaning behind the statement. Does it ring true to you? Does it open up your chest and relax your shoulders? Does it give you a full-body YES? You need to *really* believe this statement in order for it to work.

Put Your Statement into Action

Daily Reminders: I recommend writing this statement in multiple places where you'll see it every day: on your bedside table or at your desk, make it your phone's background, or set a daily reminder in the morning. You want this statement to be constantly in the forefront of your mind as you go throughout your day so that you can return to it when the noise of corporate life gets too loud.

For the next thirty days, try meditating on your aligned ambition statement each morning. After your meditation, write the statement at the top of a page, then list three to five ways you can embody it that day. Look at your schedule, your to-do list, and your commitments, and ask yourself how you can approach each one from this grounded state of being. Let this be your daily recalibration.

LEADING FROM WHOLENESS

To grow along spiritual lines means to hold a vision for ourselves beyond what our logical minds think is possible for us. In her book *Radical Acceptance*, Tara Brach says, "As we spiritually mature, our yearning to see truth and live with an open heart becomes more compelling than our reflex to avoid pain and chase after pleasure."[3] Eventually, you will crave the consistency of growing along spiritual lines rather than chastising yourself for not being perfect. It's a relief to evaluate your efforts by how much you learned, how other people were served through your work, or how much you trusted yourself.

We start to know on a deeper level what *enoughness* means to us: that we are enough, what we have is enough, and our ambition is enough to make a difference. Now imagine what's possible when you lead a project, a team, your family, or a community from *this* intention. That's what the stories in the next chapter will show you.

CHAPTER 9

BEYOND AMBITION

How Abundance, Faith, and Surrender Move Us Forward

You don't have to look far to see that we need a revolution in our leadership spaces. In our companies, in our communities, leadership is too often predicated on:

- Scarcity: a sense that there's not enough to go around, so I need to safeguard my resources.
- Certainty: believing we alone know what's right and wrong.
- Identity: separating each other into buckets that create an us-versus-them dynamic.
- Control: seeking power over others instead of building power between us.

Ambition that is informed by something greater than these is what's required to transform our organizations. That something greater is our heart, our intuition, our shared humanity.

Aligned ambition is a transformational power that can't help but stretch beyond the confines of our own lives. When we are tapped into a power greater than our fear, we've unlocked a limitless source of inspiration and leadership—fueled by service and operating on a new plane of thinking. It's likely that you want to share what you've learned and, more importantly, experienced in your life. Like when you find an incredible hack or tip that you just *have* to share with others. There are a few principles that are helpful in order to live and give aligned ambition in your organizations, communities, and families.

NON-DUAL THINKING

We are stuck in a paradigm where strength is seen as being *right* and *certain*. There seems to be no room to change our minds, embrace nuance, or allow for the gray area. I see this mindset show up in my clients every day, whether it's staying silent in meetings unless they're absolutely sure of the answer or the self-blame that follows taking a job that turned out to be a poor fit. They tell themselves they should have known better, as if certainty were a prerequisite for growth.

Our success wounds lead us to default into black-and-white thinking: believing there's a right and wrong answer, a good and bad option, or an optimal and suboptimal outcome. This limiting mindset shrouds our vision of what is possible. We know in our hearts this kind of thinking limits us, but we have a hard time changing because we fear uncertainty (that's where faith comes in).

Instead, we can embrace the ancient philosophy of non-dual thinking. Non-duality comes from the Sanskrit word *advaita*, meaning "not two." It's a way of viewing the world as interconnected, and it embraces the nuance in the gray area. A favorite phrase of any career coach is "Two things can be true at the same time."

Intelligence is holding two ideas at once. Looking at a project or a first draft and thinking, "It is enough, *and* I can work to make it better. Not because I'm afraid of what will happen if I don't keep improving it but because I want to. Because I care, because it matters to me, because I'm hooked." We can embrace our desire for a good outcome while tapping into our intrinsic motivation at the same time.

Holding two ideas at once creates common ground from which collaboration is possible. You've likely been in a situation where your perspective differs from a colleague's or a boss'. Perhaps your vision for the team or company differs from theirs. There are good ideas in both. The goal isn't for one of us to win but to create something together that's better than the sum of its parts. How can we think beyond our individual visions and create something even bigger?

If someone disagrees with a prevailing perspective, that doesn't make them evil or wrong. It means they're thinking outside the confines of groupthink, which signifies independent thinking over loyalty. Workplaces can fall into the trap of valuing conformity over nuance by shutting down different ideas and limiting dissent in subtle messaging like "We do things differently; we don't do *that here.*" Leaders who are able to hold the standard for their organization in one hand *and* the possibility that things *could* be done differently or better are able to be more innovative thinkers and better leaders.

Non-duality can also mean the unification of our three selves: integrating the darkness of our wounds into the lightness of our compassion. You've been practicing non-dual thinking in Chapter 5 as you both embrace the hurt or frustrated or judgmental parts of yourself while also desiring to move past them. In doing that for yourself, you're able to do that for others, which allows people to be both seen and motivated to change their behavior.

FAITH

Faith is the choice to believe in something that's unseen or uncertain. Non-duality requires faith. Any sort of creation, whether it's a new product launch, a new business venture, a budding friendship, or a new career path, comes from faith in what could be. Faith and trust fuel the very best things in our lives: creativity, connection, innovation, and novelty.

Throughout our careers, we will encounter moments where we can choose to leap into the unknown, guided by faith, or stay in place, stymied by fear. For example, a Hider might have to rely on her faith when she finally chooses to look at job boards for new positions and face the possibility of making a "wrong choice." A Pleaser may have to free-fall through the uncertainty of setting a new boundary or saying no, as she learns to withstand other people's disappointment. A Seeker must embrace the faith that she is exactly where she's meant to be as she focuses more on what she can contribute to her current role rather than fantasizing about what could be better.

In my experience, having taken the leap multiple times, into entrepreneurship, into starting a business overseas, into sobriety, let me tell you this: Faith can be fun. Nike founder Phil Knight has one of my favorite reflections on the subject: "There comes a time in every life when the past recedes and the future opens. It's that moment when you turn to face the unknown. Some will turn back to what they already know. Some will walk straight ahead into uncertainty. I can't tell you which one is right. But I can tell you which one is more fun."[1] Isn't that the truth?

There's a vulnerability in faith, which is why we prefer the armor of certainty. Our Protector Self craves certainty like an addict craves her fix. Our True Self prefers trust and faith to open new possibilities. Certainty is myopic. Faith is expansive. Faith is trust in action.

So which would you choose? The mundanity of certainty? Or the joyful thrill of faith?

ABUNDANCE

Abundance is the choice to recognize the enoughness within you and around you. It is the antidote to the lie of scarcity told to us by capitalism—that you need to have more, buy more, be more.

As I was writing a draft of this chapter, I was just a mile away when the Palisades wildfires broke out in Los Angeles. I was also thirty-seven weeks pregnant. We rushed through the house to pack a few essentials—a change of clothes, passports, and the dog's medicine. I took one last look at the nursery I had spent months designing, hoping that in just two weeks, our son would be arriving safely back home. We evacuated quickly and I called to check on friends and loved ones across the city.

While our home was safe, many people in our community lost their houses, their entire life's savings, and their possessions in a matter of minutes. Despite the devastation and grief, the sentiment that is shared among these friends is that even though they lost so much, nothing of true value was lost. Their community continues to show up for them, their kids' schools found new campuses, and they still have their lives. An attitude of abundance is a choice to see what remains as enough. Marianne Williamson says, "The key to abundance is meeting limited circumstances with unlimited thoughts."[2] This is not about plastering toxic positivity onto a crisis. Instead, their bravery, resilience, and perseverance are shepherding them into an unknown future that they see as hopeful and good, even though it's not the one they would have chosen.

Our careers are full of uncertainty and loss, such as layoffs, restructuring, or losing your biggest client. In response to my own career losses, my success wound will tell me that I won't recover and that I'm worse off than I was before. But while I can't control my first thought, I can choose my second thought. Meeting obstacles with limitless thinking means choosing to look for the lessons and the new opportunities that inevitably arise from unexpected circumstances. This is a big shift for Seekers, who can choose to look for the opportunities for growth and contribution in their current job instead of fixating on what's lacking or fantasizing about another job where all their career woes would vanish. Grinders can be fueled by curiosity (*I wonder what a solution to this problem looks like?*) or desire (*I want to give my all to solving this*) instead of urgency and insufficiency.

SURRENDER

I once saw someone on the beach with the word *surrender* tattooed across their inner bicep—a striking reminder of how strength is in surrender. Like many spiritual principles, there's a paradox in this concept. In spiritual terms, surrender means to align your will and actions with an intelligence greater than your own. It also means to live in acceptance of reality instead of fighting it.

Serenity also comes with surrender. The so-called Serenity Prayer that's said in unison at the beginning and end of twelve-step meetings goes, "Grant me the serenity to accept the things I cannot change, the courage to change the things I can, and the wisdom to know the difference." The ultimate act of surrender is asking for a new perspective (which you did in Chapter 6) and asking your inner knowing to guide your actions toward what you can influence.

Our power comes from knowing the line between what is in our control and what is outside it. In our careers, we may face re-orgs, layoffs, or getting a new boss we dislike. Strength is found in our ability to surrender to the reality of what is and find our own way through. The wisdom to know the difference between what we can change and what we must accept.

Throughout this book, you have learned how to surrender your wounds to an inner healer and be brave enough to set aside your old ways of working. Every step of the way, you've been surrendering, practicing faith, and embracing non-dual thinking. This will serve you well as you go out into the world as a new paradigm leader.

GIVING IT AWAY: A NEW PARADIGM OF LEADERSHIP

When my clients feel more satisfied in their lives and secure in who they are, they naturally bring this into the workplace. They become eager to share these principles with their teams and direct reports, without needing to overhaul the business model or make grand declarations. As a coach, my focus is on removing the barriers between confidence and action, enabling clients to be fully effective at work, free from self-doubt and perfectionism. What they do from there, how they implement aligned ambition at work, looks different in every context.

Changing an organization starts with changing yourself. That's what new paradigm leadership is: a radical sense of self-responsibility paired with small, intentional actions that ripple outward to those around you. This kind of leadership isn't flashy or showy, and it's not about grand-scale change management. It's about small, practical shifts that create real change, even within rigid corporate structures. Here are some examples.

EMBEDDING ALIGNED AMBITION IN PERFORMANCE REVIEWS

Hyper-growth start-ups tend to operate in a state of chaos and overwhelm, and Mei's company was no exception. Mei had spent months cultivating a new way of working outside this chaos by focusing on fewer priorities to have the greatest impact.

Mei's team was approaching another product launch, a period that usually brought incredible stress. This time, she took a different approach: aligning her team's performance reviews with individual strengths and focusing on fewer priorities. She introduced it as a pilot, explaining that evaluations would center on how effectively each person leveraged their strengths to deliver on a few key objectives.

Mei worked with each team member to identify three to four key priorities based on their unique skill set. Then she aligned incentives like their bonuses and performance reviews to how well they were able to carry out these objectives with their strengths. This sent the message to the team that Mei valued deliberate focus on a few key priorities during this product launch. She applied the principle of abundance by reassuring the team they had enough time, resources, and support to get this product shipped. Though initially met with skepticism, this pilot resulted in better collaboration and a renewed sense of purpose across the team.

Mei's example illustrates that small changes can have a large impact on team morale and motivation. Mei didn't have to change the whole company; she could influence the people and policies around her.

INSTITUTIONALIZING ECONOMIC ENOUGHNESS IN BUSINESS

Joy, the CEO of an insurance brokerage outside San Antonio, is redefining what it means to run a successful company. Rather than chasing growth for growth's sake, she leads with the principle of *economic enoughness*—ensuring her business thrives financially while serving people and the planet.

Joy shared, "For years, I poured my own intensity and fixation on 'up-and-to-the-right' growth into the business, pushing for expansion just for the sake of it. That got us far as a business. But I operated in a state of perpetual dissatisfaction. We were never big enough. There was always more the business and our leadership team could be doing. I burned out my team in the process. But when I began to examine my definition of *enoughness*, I knew we had to bring this definition into the business, too. What's the point of owning and running a business if it makes everyone miserable?"

Joy made two small changes that created a large impact.

Joy's insurance brokerage works primarily with rural farming communities in Texas. She recognizes the web of networks her business touches: employees, clients, partner insurers, and the wider San Antonio community. Joy had her team do an audit of their insurance partners, choosing partners who align with her values and encouraging clients to consider policies that strengthen community resilience, such as disaster preparedness or sustainable rebuilding coverage.

Second, she tracked employee satisfaction, retention, and the firm's environmental footprint, weaving these values-driven metrics into leadership accountability. The result speaks for itself: Her brokerage achieved a 140 percent year-over-year profit increase while also improving employee retention.

By aligning her brokerage with new principles, Joy demonstrates that even in a traditional industry, companies can practice economic enoughness and thrive. This is the epitome of non-dual thinking—we can pursue profit and impact simultaneously—and abundance in action. Her story reminds us that when leaders put people and community alongside profit, they build businesses that are not only financially sound but also deeply purposeful.

PARENTING WITH WHOLENESS

Many of my clients are also parents who grapple with an important question: How can we equip our children to handle real-world challenges without perpetuating outdated, success-wounded thinking? This is a complex question, one that I've been considering deeply.

I've written most of this book while pregnant and now parenting my first child. My husband and I have discussed how to help him discover what he loves to do without creating the pressure that there's one "perfect" career path for him. We want him to be motivated and hardworking, but not to see his worth solely in terms of productivity. More than ever I've had to confront my own success wound and consider how I am practicing the principles in this book—not only for myself but also as an example for my son.

A few of my clients have practiced these tools with their children, even at a young age. You can invite them into conversations about their emotions and create moments when they can sit with uncomfortable feelings like frustration or sadness without the fear of judgment. You can help them to reframe their thinking toward possibility with simple Power Questions. You can model ways of working, including boundaries that honor your values. These simple actions done repeatedly will help nurture the authenticity of your children while supporting their inner strength and confidence in the process.

Finally, I've also seen clients turn their aligned ambition statements from Chapter 8 into a guiding values statement for their family. For example, Joy's aligned ambition statement is: *My success comes from living my values of service, resilience, and respect for myself and others.* She modeled how service can be expressed as a family value. She helps her children realize that their contributions matter—whether it's lending a neighbor a hand, volunteering time at a local shelter, or simply being present for a friend in need. This cultivates empathy, compassion, and a sense of belonging, allowing her children to understand their place in the broader tapestry of their community.

A LOVE LETTER TO AMBITIOUS WOMEN

The question we've explored throughout our time together is *What do you really want?* Your ambition is your creative force, and you get to choose what you do with it.

So let me ask you now: What do you really want to do with your ambition?

When I ask my clients this question, regardless of their background, country, or position, they all say a variation of the same thing. They want connection.

"I want to work with like-minded people."

"To collaborate and create with others."

"To have a great boss who mentors me."

"To be connected with the mission and the values of the company."

"To make a good living to take care of my loved ones."

Connection gives our lives meaning. We overcomplicate job satisfaction, analyzing if we are in the "right" job or on the "right" career path. But fulfillment is more about *how* we work than what we *do* for work. With connection as a North Star, we can shape a career and life that reflects the connections we value—connection to a mission, to our colleagues, to an inspiring intellectual pursuit, and more.

If we're going to take anyone's advice when it comes to creating a vision for our lives, it's Oprah's. She says, "The most important question you can ask yourself is 'What do I really want?'... And when you do that, the forces of life rise up to meet you. The reason why most people live such chaotic lives is because they are living in chaos in their heads. As soon as you get clear, it clears up."[3] When our ambition comes to serve this vision, we are unstoppable. The path is made clear.

Walking forward with faith, an attitude of abundance, and a practice of surrendering to reality, your career suddenly becomes more than just a job. It's a way of being in a world where your authenticity is reflected in everything that you do. Who wouldn't want to work alongside someone with this devotion and inspiration? Who wouldn't be attracted to the vision of someone who was so clear on who they are, what they want, and why it matters? Your leadership naturally shines through from this state of clarity.

Sure, you're going to forget to reframe a negative thought or slip back into old habits like pleasing people or numbing out in ways you're not proud of. You're human and you're perfectly imperfect. I don't care if you fall off track. But I do care about the rate at which you come back to yourself. There isn't an ultimate destination, nor is there an end to healing your success wound. Rather, it's an ongoing choice to see your worth as inherent and within rather than conditional and earned. This is my greatest wish for you, for me, and for all of us.

ACKNOWLEDGMENTS

This book has the good fortune of being believed in, lovingly edited, and cheered on by hundreds of people.

To my agents Mia Vitale and Sarah Passick, thank you for totally getting this idea from the start, championing it, and shepherding it through its publishing process. You never dropped a ball, probably because you're both Grinders. I can't thank you enough for your partnership and can't wait for more.

Thank you to Renee Sedliar for your expert edits and your care in taking this book all the way across the finish line. Thank you to Lauren Marino for your early feedback that, to me, had the impact of an MFA in an email. Thank you also to Niyati Patel and the rest of the team at Hachette and Grand Central Balance for all that you've done to bring *Healing the Success Wound* to the world!

Lisa Weinert, thank you for being in the trenches with me every single step of the way. Thank you for being my creative mentor and friend for the last ten years. From late-night calls in Paris to holding me as I hobbled across the finish line thirty-seven weeks pregnant in the middle of the LA fires. You believed in me and this message in all the moments that mattered.

Liz Keenan, thank you for your thorough and thoughtful feedback to take this book from good to great.

Thank you to my early readers who celebrated what worked on the page and lovingly critiqued what could be improved. You made me a better writer and helped me say what I want to say exactly how I wanted to say it: Sarah Levy, Jenny Lintz, Lauren Brown, Alex Ostebo. Thank you also to Maddie Hendricks and Michael Lewen for your creative mentorship and the endless calls about covers and titles. And to Brielle Friedman for inspiring me with your creative approach to life and dear friendship.

Jenny Wood, thank you for being in the trenches with me during this book launch. Thank you for your mentorship, guidance, and believing in me and this book!

Thank you to everyone who has opened up their network, taken my call, brought me to speak to their company, given me advice, and spent time to support me and this book. I'm grateful to be a beneficiary of your valuable time and energy. Special thanks to Lea Prohov and Sara Waters for your brainstorming and marketing ideas. I'm lucky to have you two as my original work wives.

Jess Geist, I'm so grateful that my very specific "wanted" ad for a coach led me to you. Thank you for helping shape so many of these concepts and frameworks, and for teaching me how to be a coach with both integrity and business acumen.

To all my teachers, mentors, coaches, and therapists who picked me up and dusted me off so I could keep going. Your insights and lessons are all over this book.

To my Finally Fulfilled ladies—you shaped how I teach these methods with your willingness to experiment with finding an inner solution to your career. You have been so generous with your feedback and how you've championed this work. I love each of you!

To my dear clients, thank you for sharing your hopes, dreams, light, and shadows with me. It's such a privilege to work with you. Thank you for trusting me.

Mary Ruth Quinn, you held a vision for my life before I could see it. I am who I am today because of you.

There aren't enough words to thank my dearest friends. You have lived the stories in this book alongside me. You've celebrated my wins as your own. That kind of friendship is rare and one of my greatest blessings: my Green Couch, my Google Gals, my Aussie Mates, and LA Ladies.

Lauren B, Lisa T, Leslie E, and Courtney T, thank you for giving me a design for living that works.

My fierce and feisty little cavvy, Paloma. You wrote every single page curled up next to me, and I love every single piece of fur on your head.

Everyone knows I hit the in-law jackpot. To the MacNeils—John, Diana, Laura, Nick, Michael, and Katy—and to Sydney Taylor. Thank you for cheering me on through every step of this process.

Phil and Ace, I love being your sister. Thank you for putting up with my overbearing older-sister habits and always knowing how to make me laugh. I love you both so much.

James, you're my greatest gift in this life. Thank you for always reminding me that I can't write a book about the success wound from my own success wound. Thank you for holding my vision when I couldn't see it anymore. I love our life together.

Crosby, you are perfect. Your cheeks and giggles and how you change every day delights me to no end. I can't wait to watch you grow up.

Dad, I know you were with me in spirit every step of the way. I see so much of you in Crosby. Thank you for my ambition, my work ethic, and for my love of all things French. I miss you every day.

Finally, to my mom, Melanie. My love of books comes from you. My spiritual curiosity comes from you. My conception of unconditional love comes from you. Thank you for everything you do and have done for me.

NOTES

Introduction

1. Field, Emily, Alexis Krivkovich, Sandra Kügele, Nicole Robinson, and Lareina Yee. (2023). *Women in the Workplace.* McKinsey & Company. https://www.mckinsey.com/featured-insights/diversity-and-inclusion/women-in-the-workplace.
2. Pudrovska, T., and A. Karraker. (2014). "Gender, Job Authority, and Depression." *Journal of Health and Social Behavior* 55(4):424–441. https://doi.org/10.1177/0022146514555223.
3. "Size of the Training Industry." (2021). Training Industry, https://trainingindustry.com/wiki/learning-services-and-outsourcing/size-of-training-industry/.
4. PwC. (2024). Global Workforce Hopes and Fears Survey. PwC. https://www.pwc.com/gx/en/issues/workforce/hopes-and-fears.html.
5. Wallace, Jennifer Breheny. (2023). *Never Enough: When Achievement Culture Becomes Toxic—and What We Can Do About It.* New York: Portfolio/Penguin.

Chapter 1: Never Enough

1. Li, Allen, Malala Lin, Allan Schweyer, and Selcuk Eren. (2023). "Job Satisfaction 2023: US Worker Satisfaction Continues to Increase." Conference Board.
2. Foster, Cynthia Ewell, Adam Horowitz, Alvin Thomas, Kiel Opperman, Polly Gipson, Amanda Burnside, Deborah M. Stone, and Cheryl A. King. (2017). "Connectedness to Family, School, Peers, and Community in Socially Vulnerable Adolescents." *Children and Youth Services Review* 81:321–331. https://doi.org/10.1016/j.childyouth.2017.08.011.
3. Wallace, Jennifer Breheny. (2019). "Students in High-Achieving Schools Are Now Named an 'At-Risk' Group, Study Says." *Washington Post.*

https://www.washingtonpost.com/lifestyle/2019/09/26/students-high-achieving-schools-are-now-named-an-at-risk-group/.

4. Schwartz, Richard C., and Martha Sweezy. (2019). *Internal Family Systems Therapy* (2nd ed.). New York: Guilford Press.
5. Celniker, Jared B., Andrew Gregory, Hyunjin J. Koo, Paul K. Piff, Peter H. Ditto, and Azim F. Shariff. (2023). "The Moralization of Effort." *Journal of Experimental Psychology: General* 152(1):60–79. https://doi.org/10.1037/xge0001259.
6. Thompson, Derek. (2019). "Workism Is Making Americans Miserable." *The Atlantic.*
7. Markovits, Daniel. (2019). *The Meritocracy Trap: How America's Foundational Myth Feeds Inequality, Dismantles the Middle Class, and Devours the Elite.* New York: Penguin Press.
8. Hersey, Tricia. (2022). "Rest Is Anything That Connects Your Mind and Body." Nap Ministry. https://thenapministry.wordpress.com/2022/02/21/rest-is-anything-that-connects-your-mind-and-body.
9. Kalleberg, A. L., and P. V. Marsden. (2019). "Work Values in the United States: Age, Period, and Generational Differences." *Annals of the American Academy of Political and Social Science* 682(1):43–59. doi: 10.1177/0002716218822291.
10. Horovitz, Bruce. (2023). "New AARP Report Finds Family Caregivers Provide $600 Billion in Unpaid Care Across the U.S." AARP. https://www.aarp.org/caregiving/financial-legal/unpaid-caregivers-provide-billions-in-care/.
11. Fry, Richard, and Carolina Aragão. (2025). "Gender Pay Gap in U.S. Has Narrowed Slightly over 2 Decades." Pew Research Center. https://www.pewresearch.org/short-reads/2025/03/04/gender-pay-gap-in-us-has-narrowed-slightly-over-2-decades/.
12. Kochhar, Rakesh. (2023). "The Enduring Grip of the Gender Pay Gap." Pew Research Center. https://www.pewresearch.org/social-trends/2023/03/01/the-enduring-grip-of-the-gender-pay-gap/.
13. Delacruz, A. Y., and A. B. Speer. (2023). "Maternal Wall Biases and the Maybe Baby Effect." *Industrial and Organizational Psychology* 16(2):221–224. doi:10.1017/iop.2023.3.
14. Maté, Gabor, and Daniel Maté. (2023). *The Myth of Normal: Trauma, Illness, and Healing in a Toxic Culture.* New York: Avery.

15. Sull, Donald, Charles Sull, William Cipolli, and Caio Brighenti. (2022). "Why Every Leader Needs to Worry About Toxic Culture." *MIT Sloan Management Review.* https://sloanreview.mit.edu/article/why-every-leader-needs-to-worry-about-toxic-culture/.
16. McKinsey & Company. (2024). *Women in the Workplace.* https://www.mckinsey.com/featured-insights/diversity-and-inclusion/women-in-the-workplace.
17. Huecker, M. R., J. Shreffler, P. T. McKeny, and D. Davis. "Imposter Phenomenon." [Updated July 31, 2023]. In: StatPearls [Internet]. Treasure Island, FL: StatPearls Publishing; January 2024. https://www.ncbi.nlm.nih.gov/books/NBK585058/.
18. Hammond, Kelsey Eyre. (2023). "Despite Professional Successes Many Women Still Experience Imposter Syndrome." Survey Center on American Life. https://www.americansurveycenter.org/women-are-achieving-greater-professional-success-yet-self-doubt-is-common/.
19. Tulshyan, Ruchika, and Jodi-Ann Burey. (2021). "Stop Telling Women They Have Imposter Syndrome." *Harvard Business Review.* https://hbr.org/2021/02/stop-telling-women-they-have-imposter-syndrome.
20. Maslach, C., and S. E. Jackson. (1981). *Maslach Burnout Inventory Manual.* Palo Alto, CA: Consulting Psychologists Press.
21. McKinsey & Company. (2021). *Women in the Workplace.* https://www.mckinsey.com/~/media/mckinsey/featured%20insights/diversity%20and%20inclusion/women%20in%20the%20workplace%202021/women-in-the-workplace-2021.pdf.
22. Hewitt, P. L., and G. L. Flett. (1990). "Perfectionism and Depression: A Multidimensional Analysis." *Journal of Social Behavior & Personality* 5(5):423–438.
23. Aguinis, Herman, and Ernest O'Boyle Jr. (2012). "The Best and the Rest: Revisiting the Norm of Normality in Individual Performance," *Personal Psychology* 65(1):79–119. https://doi.org/10.1111/j.1744-6570.2011.01239.x.
24. "Mental Health at Work." (2022). World Health Organization. https://www.who.int/news-room/fact-sheets/detail/mental-health-at-work.
25. "How Anxiety Can Be Helpful." (2024). Cleveland Clinic. https://health.clevelandclinic.org/benefits-of-anxiety.

26. Barnard, Jayne W. (2008). "Narcissism, Over-Optimism, Fear, Anger, and Depression: The Interior Lives of Corporate Leaders." *University of Cincinnati Law Review*, William & Mary Law School Research Paper No. 08-10. https://ssrn.com/abstract=1136888.
27. Hollington-Sawyer, Stephanie. (2017). "Opioids and Universal Experience of Addiction by Dr. Gabor Maté." https://drgabormate.com/opioids-universal-experience-addiction/.
28. Van Bael, K., M. Ball, J. Scarfo, and E. Suleyman. (2023). "Assessment of the Mind-Body Connection: Preliminary Psychometric Evidence for a New Self-Report Questionnaire." *BMC Psychology* 11(1):309. doi: 10.1186/s40359-023-01302-3.

Chapter 3: The Wounded Self, Protector Self, and True Self

1. Murdock, Maureen. (2020). *The Heroine's Journey: Woman's Quest for Wholeness*. Boulder, CO: Shambhala Publications.
2. Rusnak, Kari. (2020). "The Magic Ratio: The Key to Relationship Satisfaction." Gottman Institute. https://www.gottman.com/blog/the-magic-ratio-the-key-to-relationship-satisfaction/.
3. Hanson, Rick. (2013). *Hardwiring Happiness: The New Brain Science of Contentment, Calm, and Confidence*. New York: Harmony Books.
4. Graduate, Stanford. (2014). "Oprah Winfrey: The Secret of My Success." YouTube. https://www.youtube.com/watch?v=fohCkaIhnBc.
5. Williamson, Marianne. (2012). *The Law of Divine Compensation*. New York: HarperCollins.
6. Campbell, Joseph, and Bill D. Moyers. (1988) 2012. *The Power of Myth*. New York: Turtleback Books.
7. Jobs, Steve. (2005). "Stanford University Commencement Address." Stanford University, California.
8. Duke University—The Fuqua School of Business. (2013). "Apple CEO Tim Cook on Intuition." YouTube. https://www.youtube.com/watch?v=c6X9-br—jM.

Chapter 4: Aligned Ambition

1. Bradshaw, Emma L., James H. Conigrave, Ben A. Steward, Kelly A. Ferber, Philip D. Parker, and Richard M. Ryan. (2023). "A Meta-Analysis of the Dark Side of the American Dream: Evidence for the Universal

Wellness Costs of Prioritizing Extrinsic over Intrinsic Goals." *Journal of Personality and Social Psychology* 124(4):873–899.

2. Kanten, Pelin, and Murat Yesiltas. (2015). "The Effects of Positive and Negative Perfectionism on Work Engagement, Psychological Well-Being and Emotional Exhaustion." *Procedia Economics and Finance*, 23:1367–1375, ISSN 2212-5671. https://doi.org/10.1016/S2212-5671(15)00522-5.
3. Kegan, Robert. (1982). *The Evolving Self: Problem and Process in Human Development*. Cambridge, MA: Harvard University Press.

Chapter 5: A New Way of Feeling

1. Jung, C. G. (1959). *Aion: Researches into the Phenomenology of the Self.* Translated by R. F. C. Hull. Vol. 9, Part 2 of *The Collected Works of C. G. Jung.* Princeton, NJ: Princeton University Press.
2. Rogers, Carl R. (1961). *On Becoming a Person: A Therapist's View of Psychotherapy.* Boston: Houghton Mifflin.
3. "Dr. Herbert Benson's Relaxation Response." (n.d.). *Psychology Today.* https://www.psychologytoday.com/intl/blog/heart-and-soul-healing/201303/dr-herbert-benson-s-relaxation-response.
4. Brach, Tara. (2003). *Radical Acceptance: Embracing Your Life with the Heart of a Buddha*. New York: Bantam Dell.

Chapter 6: A New Way of Thinking

1. Alpert, Joseph S. (2025). "A Selection of Fascinating Facts About the Brain and Heart." *American Journal of Medicine* 138(6):921–922. https://doi.org/10.1016/j.amjmed.2024.11.017.
2. Hirsch, C. R., D. M. Clark, and A. Mathews. (2006). "Imagery and Interpretations in Social Phobia: Support for the Combined Cognitive Biases Hypothesis." *Behavioral Therapy* 37(3):223–236. https://www.sciencedirect.com/science/article/abs/pii/S0005789406000402. doi: 10.1016/j.beth.2006.02.001.
3. Bethune, Sophie. (2022). "More than a Quarter of U.S. Adults Say They're So Stressed They Can't Function." American Psychological Association. https://www.apa.org/news/press/releases/2022/10/multiple-stressors-no-function.
4. Katie, Byron, and Stephen Mitchell. (2008). *Loving What Is.* New York: Random House.

Chapter 7: A New Way of Working

1. Miller, Monica. "Cognitive Dissonance Theory (Festinger)." Accessed November 1, 2024. https://www.researchgate.net/profile/Monica-Miller/publication/291356571_Cognitive_Dissonance_Theory_Festinger/links/56a292d808ae1b65112cb965/Cognitive-Dissonance-Theory-Festinger.pdf.
2. Bem, Daryl J. (1972). "Self-Perception Theory." *Advances in Experimental Social Psychology* 6(6):1–62. https://doi.org/10.1016/s0065-2601(08)60024-6.
3. Duhigg, Charles. (2012). *Power of Habit: Why We Do What We Do in Life and Business.* New York: Random House Trade Paperbacks.
4. Uncapher, Melina R., and Anthony D. Wagner. (2018). "Minds and Brains of Media Multitaskers: Current Findings and Future Directions." *Proceedings of the National Academy of Sciences* 115(40):9889–9896. https://doi.org/10.1073/pnas.1611612115.
5. Rosenberg, Marshall B. (2015). *Nonviolent Communication: A Language of Life* (3rd ed.). Encinitas, CA: PuddleDancer Press.
6. Rosenberg, M. (2003). *Nonviolent Communication: A Language of Life: Life-Changing Tools for Healthy Relationships* (2nd ed.). Culver City, CA: PuddleDancer Press.
7. Hendricks, Gay. (2009). *The Big Leap.* New York: HarperCollins.

Chapter 8: Leading from Wholeness

1. Schucman, Helen. (1992). *A Course in Miracles.* Glen Ellen, CA: Foundation for Inner Peace.
2. Duckworth, Angela. (2016). *Grit: The Power of Passion and Perseverance.* New York: Scribner.
3. Brach, Tara. (2003). *Radical Acceptance: Embracing Your Life with the Heart of a Buddha.* New York: Bantam Dell.

Chapter 9: Beyond Ambition

1. Brettman, Allan. (2011). "Knight Management Center Allows Nike Chairman to Revel in His Day." *Oregon Live.* https://www.oregonlive.com/playbooksandprofits/2011/05/knight_management_center_allow.html.

2. Williamson, Marianne. (2012). *The Law of Divine Compensation*. New York: HarperCollins.
3. *The Daily Show with Trevor Noah*. "Oprah Winfrey—'The Path Made Clear.'" Interview by Trevor Noah. Aired April 17, 2019, on Comedy Central.

INDEX